Watercolor Art Collection

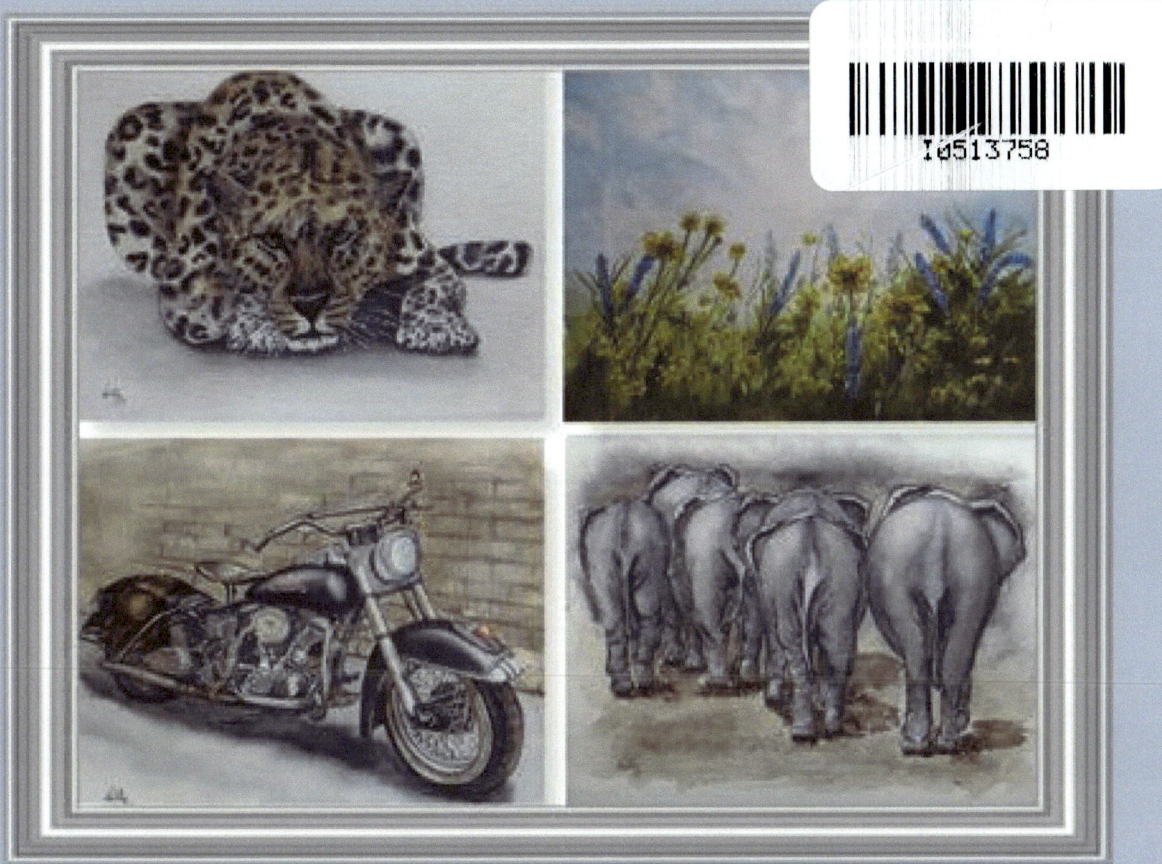

Paintings By Kelly Mills

Dedicated to my daughter Mellina

Check out Fine Art America for prints of these Original Watercolor Paintings!

Visit: Kelly Mills Fine Art Amercia

ISBN 9798704354048   COPYRIGHT @ 2021 KELLY MILLS All Rights Reserved

Horses Beauty

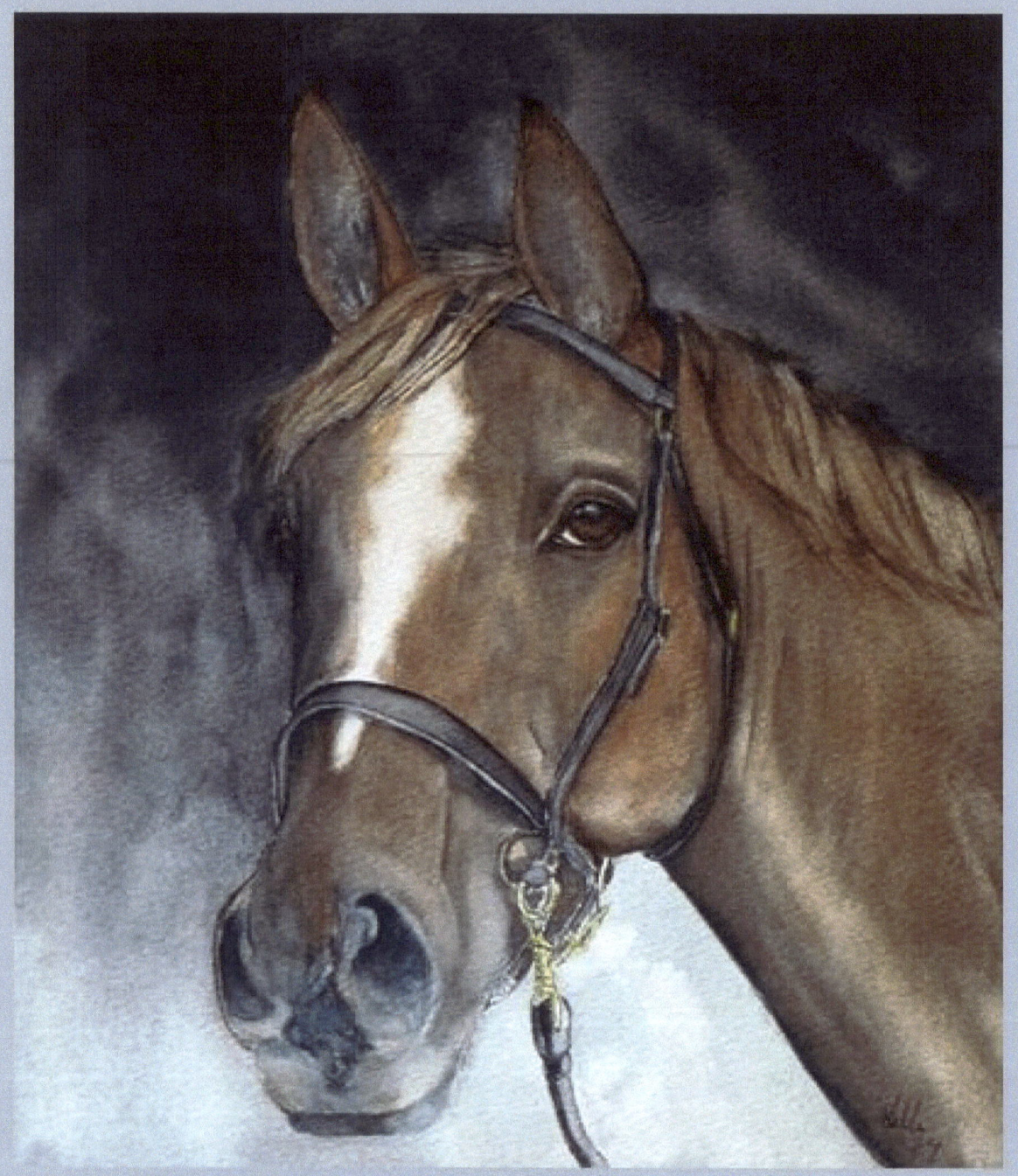

Original 11"x 14" Watercolor

Lurking Tiger

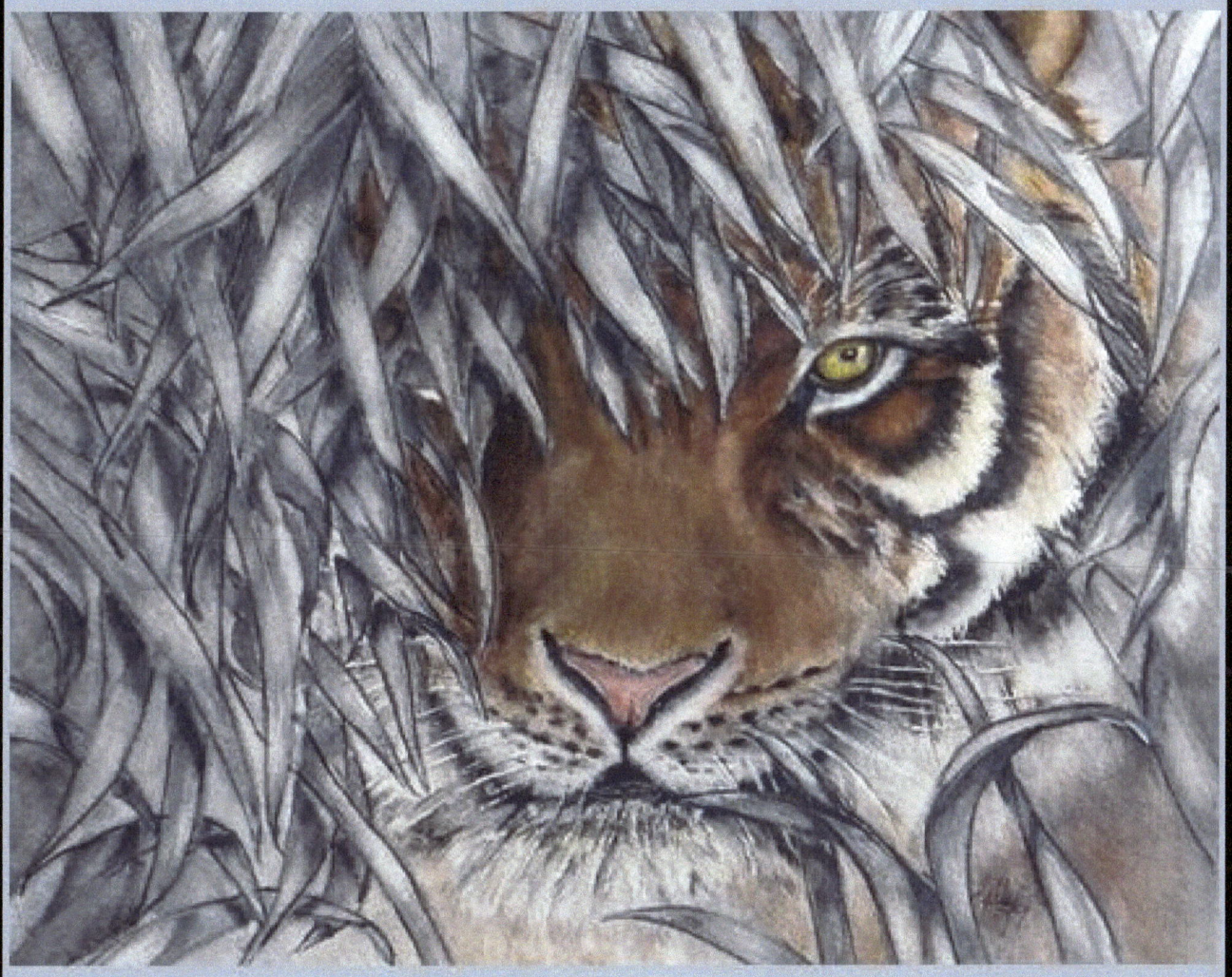

Original 14"x 11" Watercolor

Rome's Colosseum

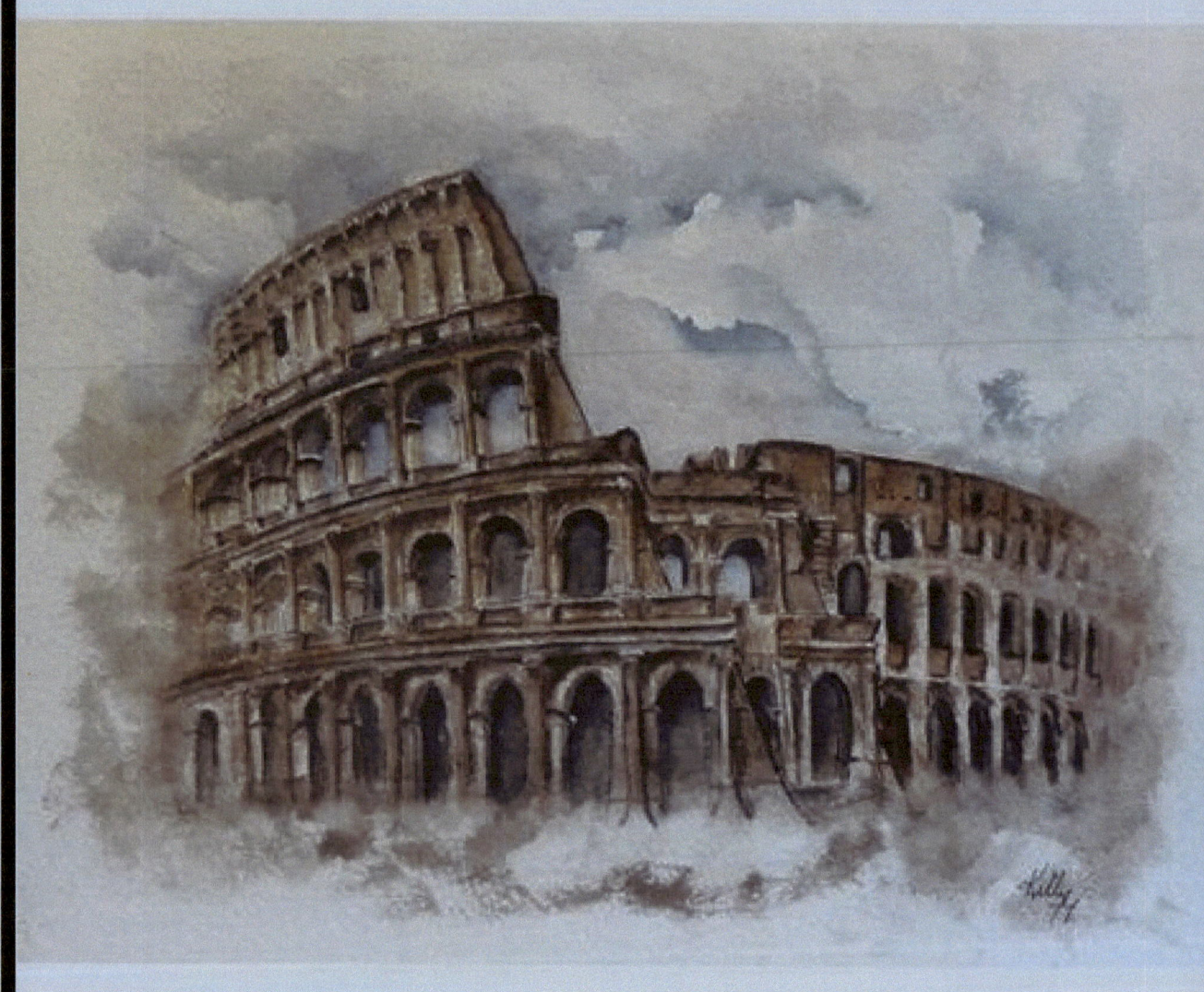

Original 14"x 11" Watercolor

Palm Cockatoo

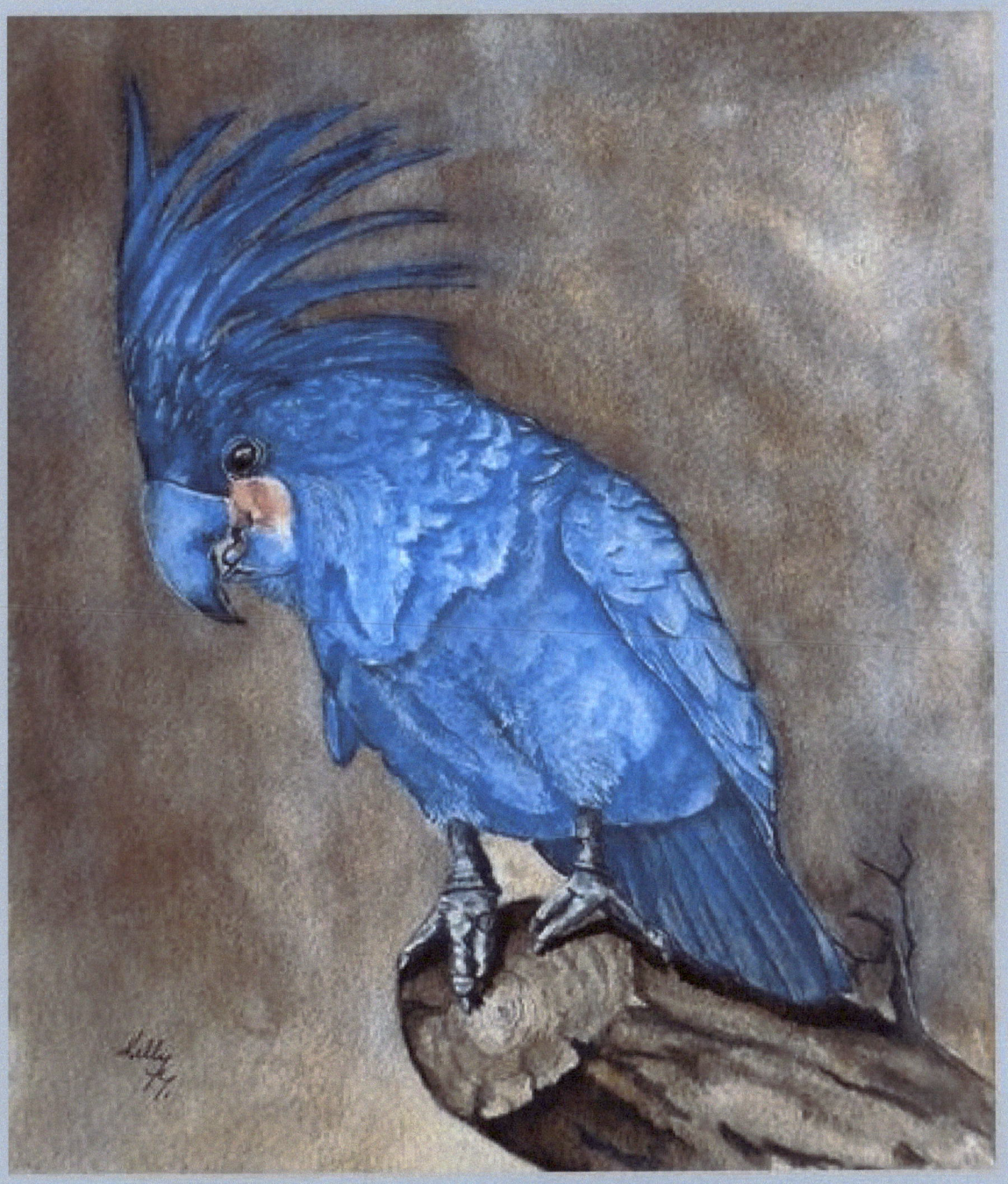

Original 11"x 14" Watercolor

Old Piano Keys

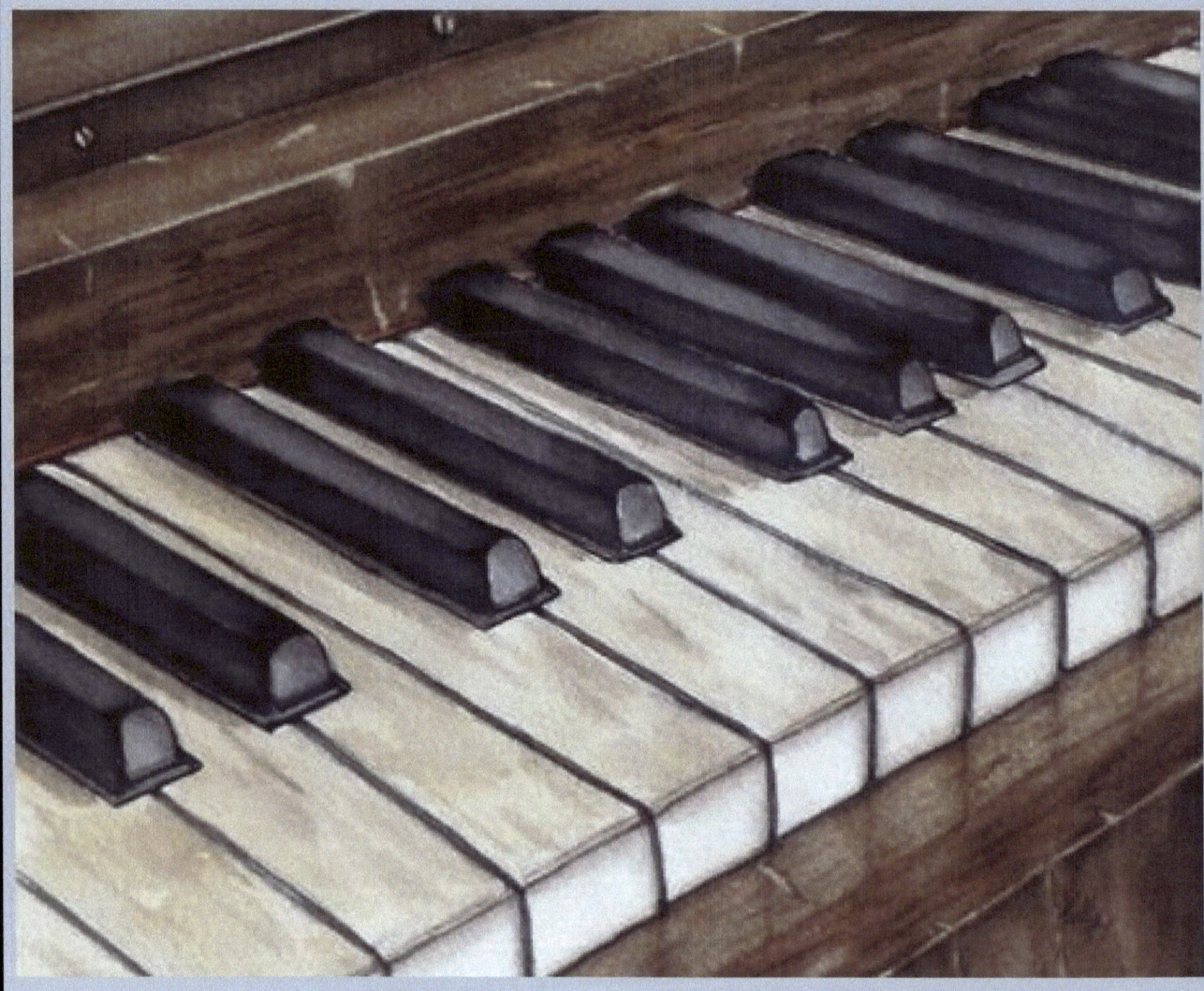

Original 14"x 11" Watercolor

Crashing Ocean's Wave

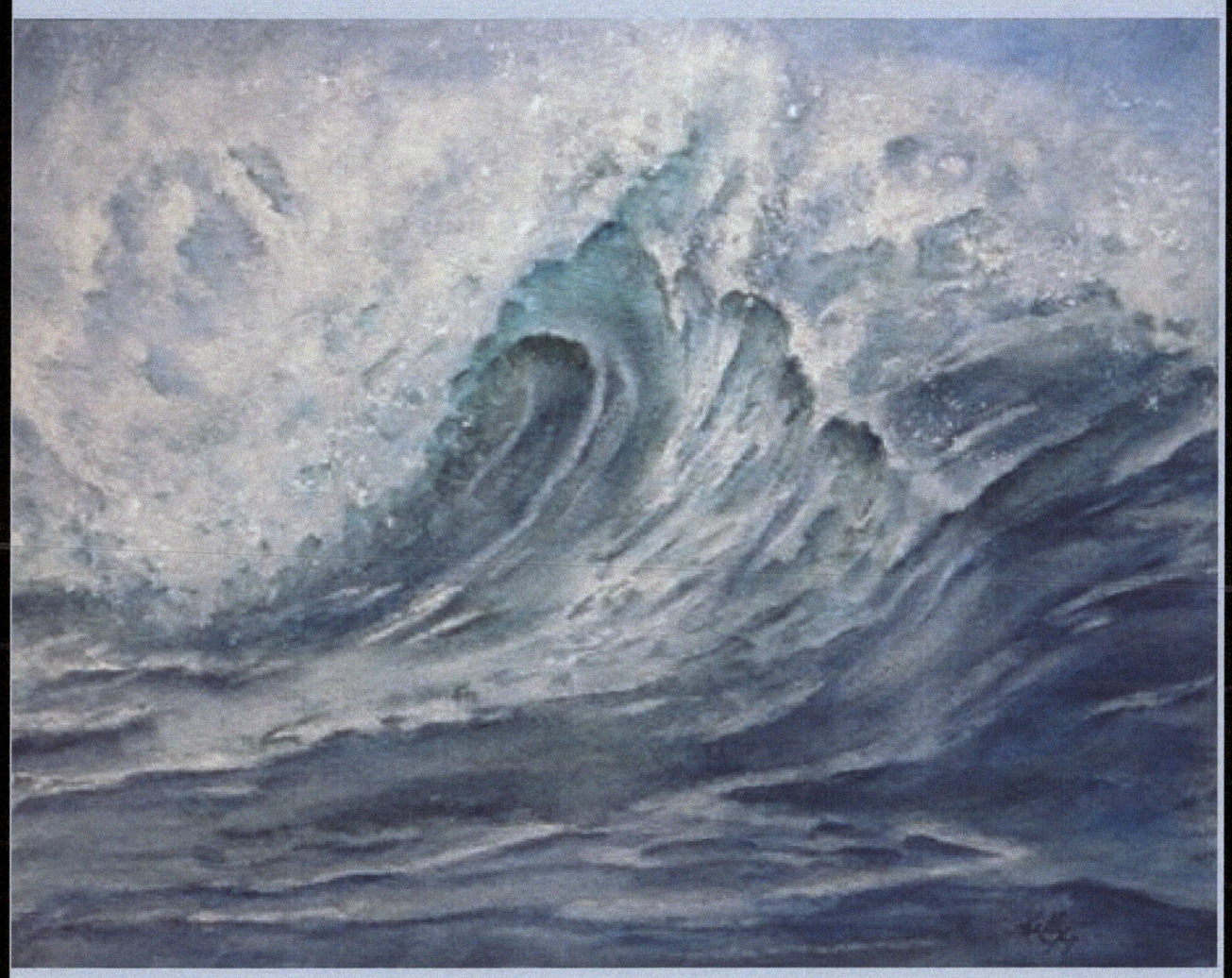

Original 14"x 11" Watercolor

Prowling Leopard

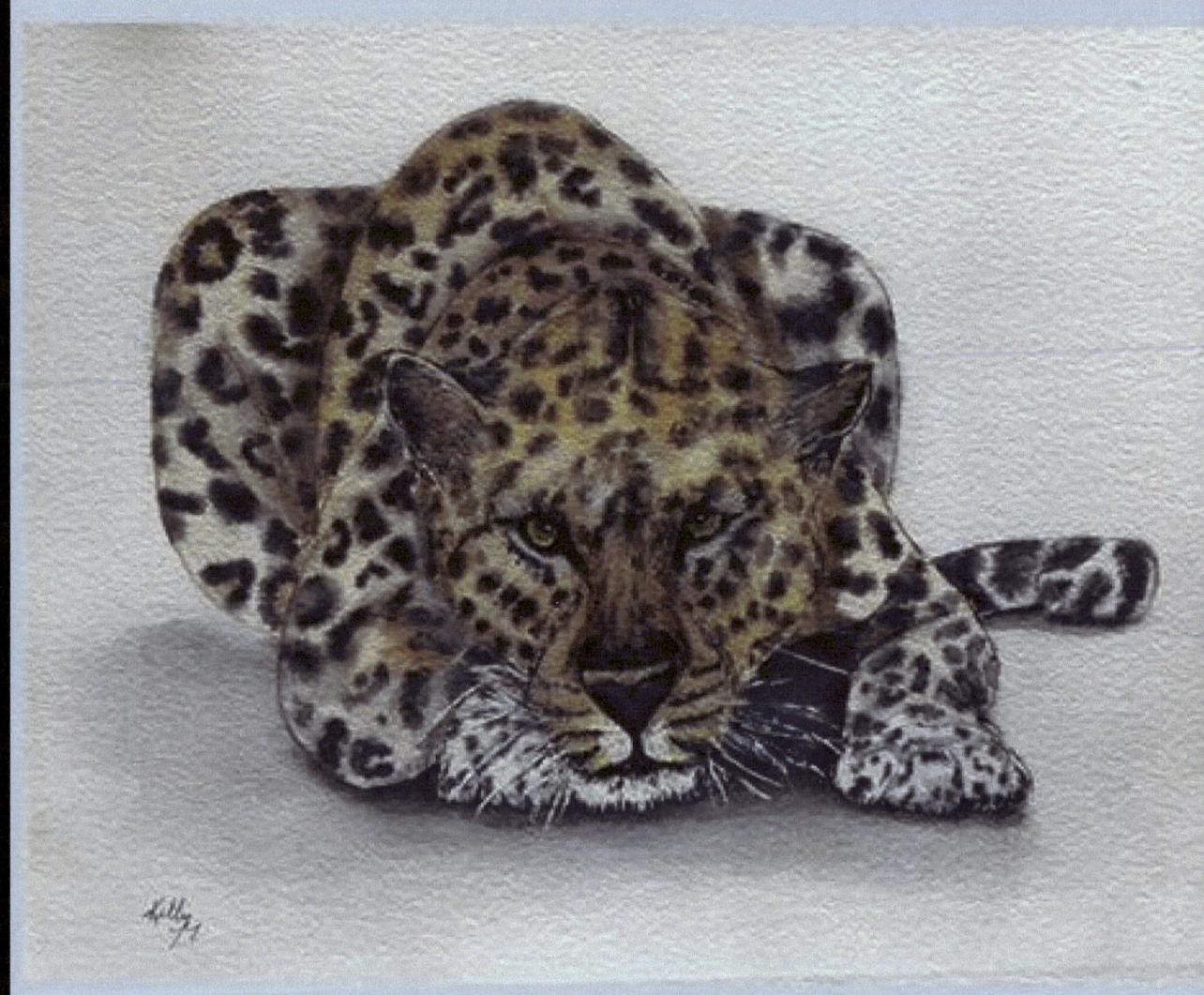

Original 14"x 11" Watercolor

"The Cry"

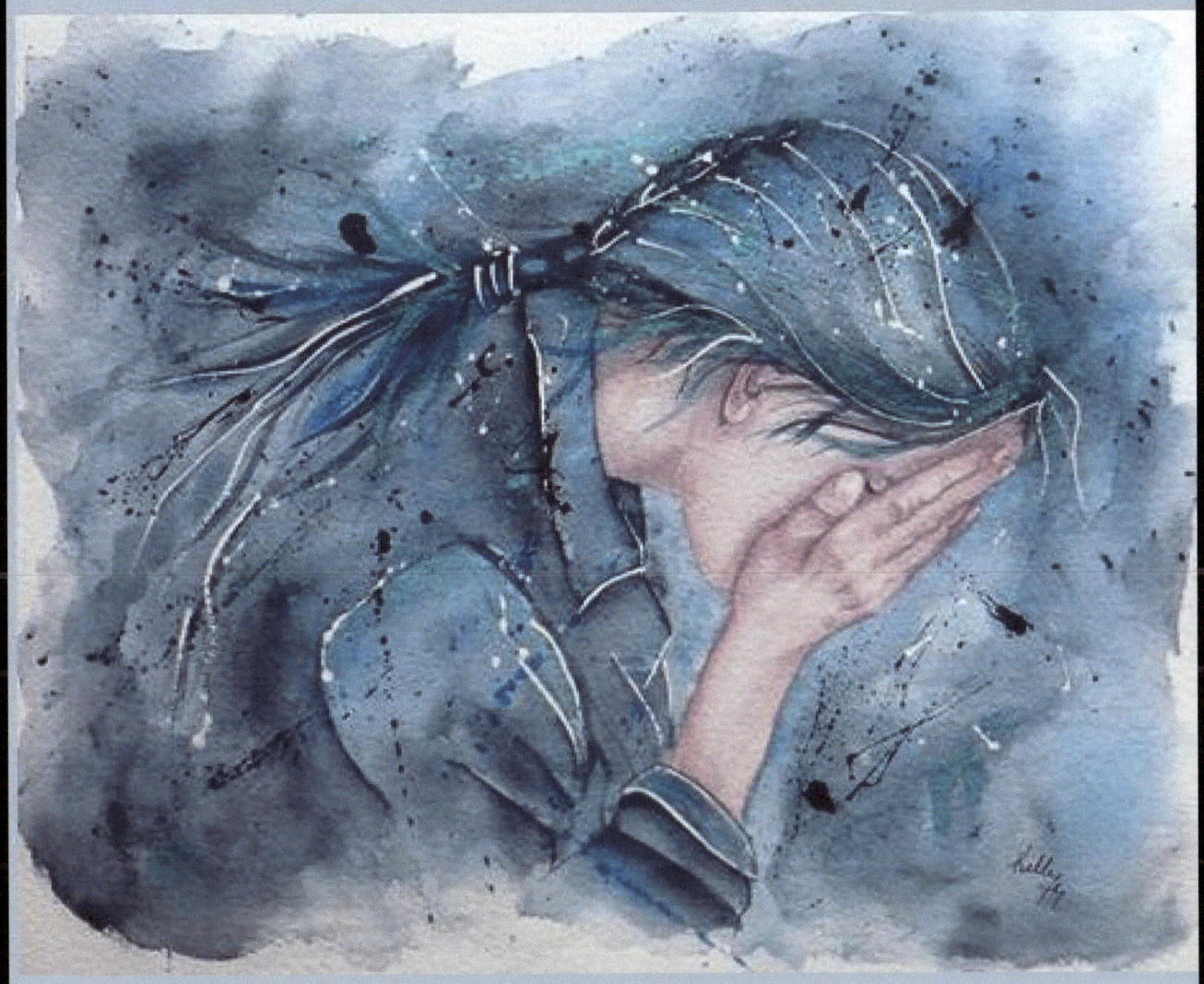

Original 14"x 11" Watercolor

Cobblestone Walk

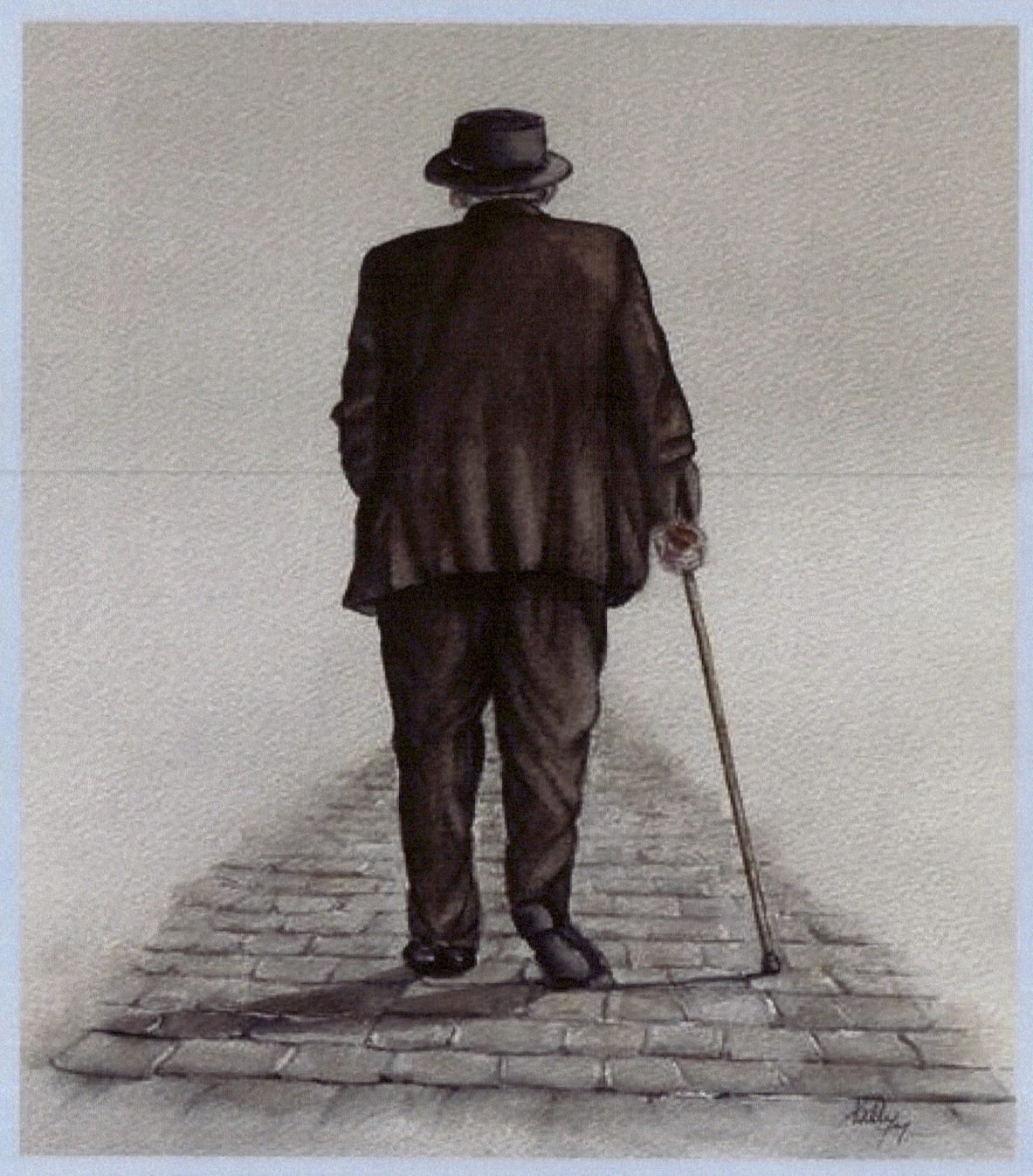

Original 11"x 14" Watercolor

Reaching for Spring

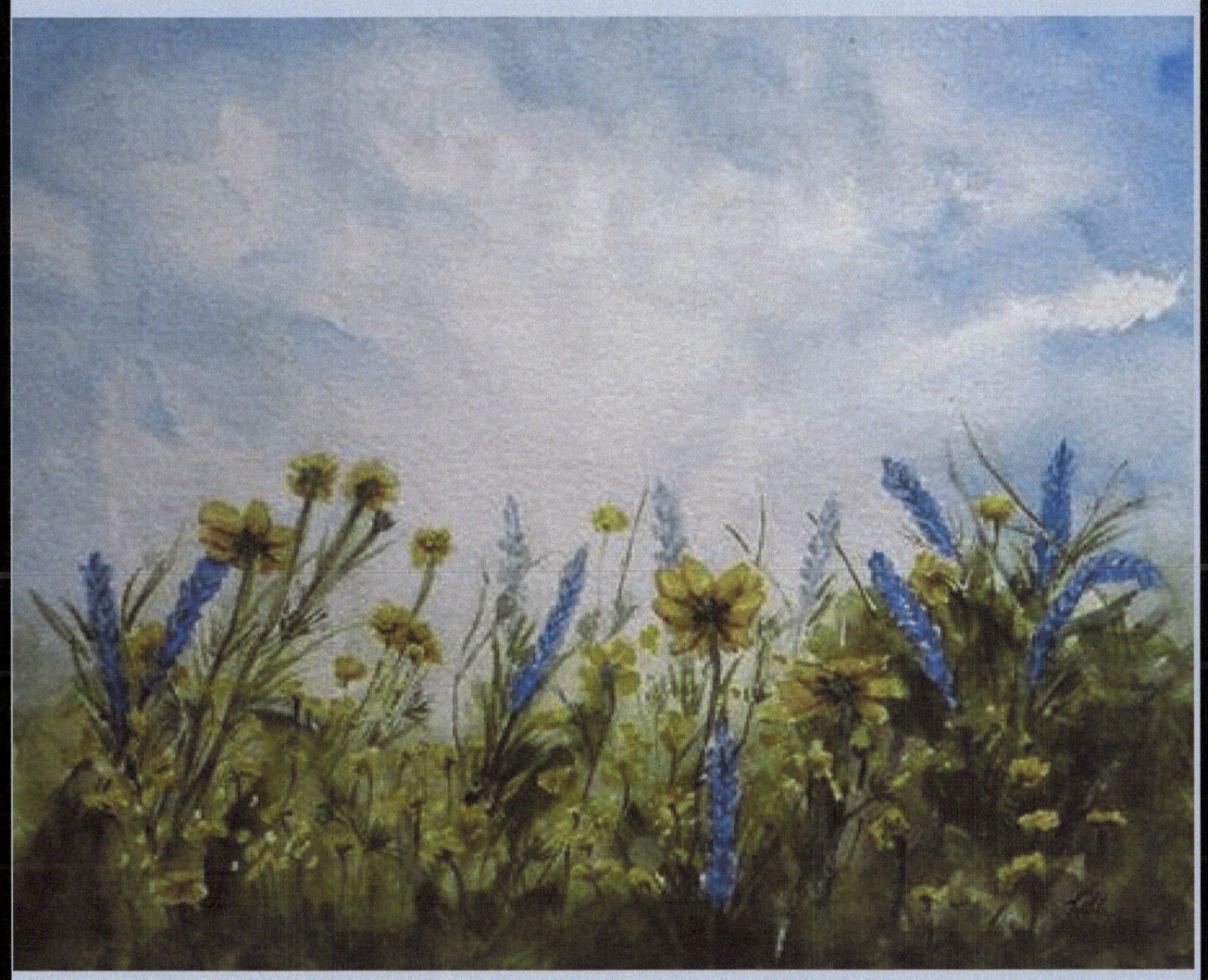

Original 14"x 11" Watercolor

Vintage Saddle Shoes

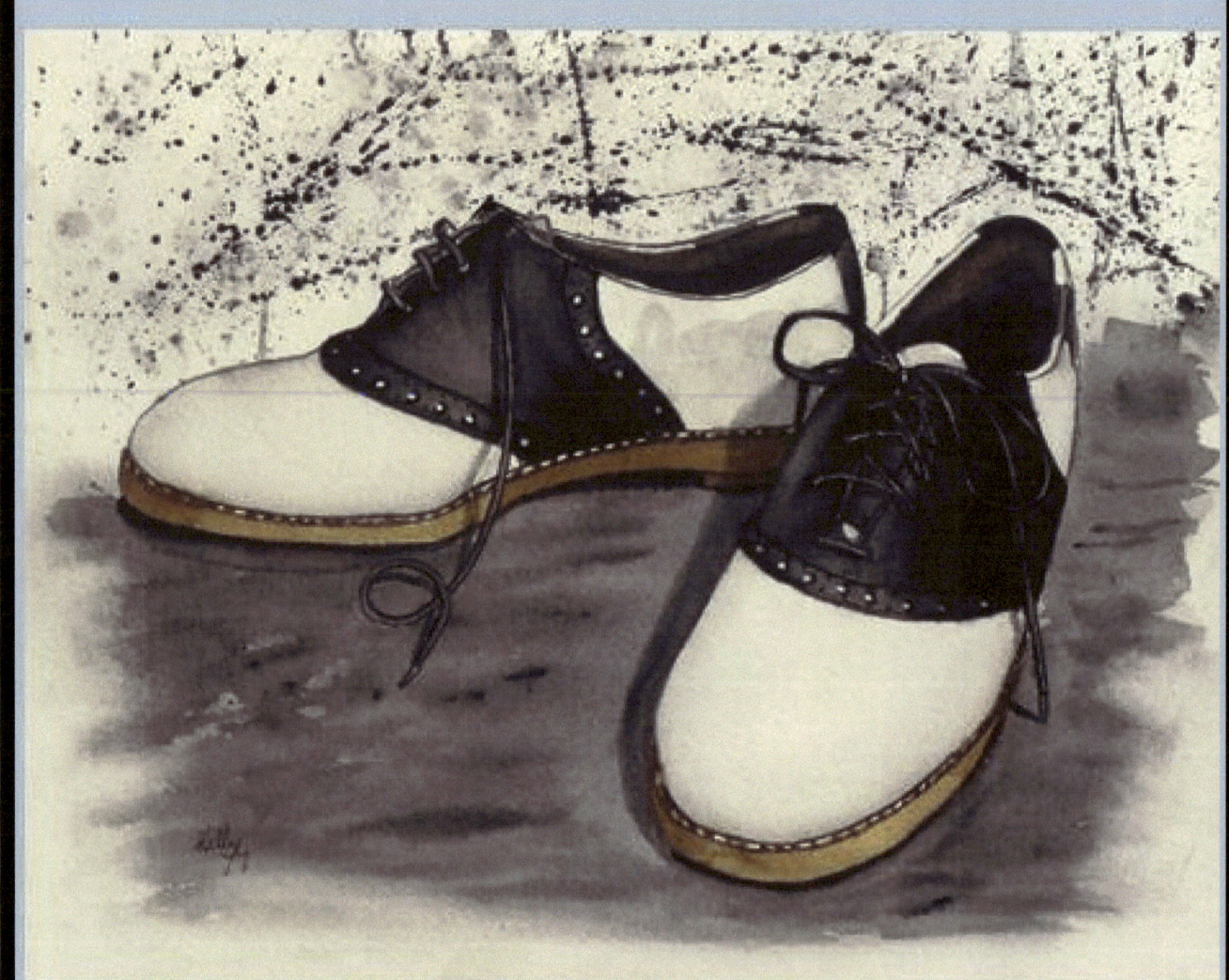

Original 14"x 11" Watercolor

Elephant Leaving

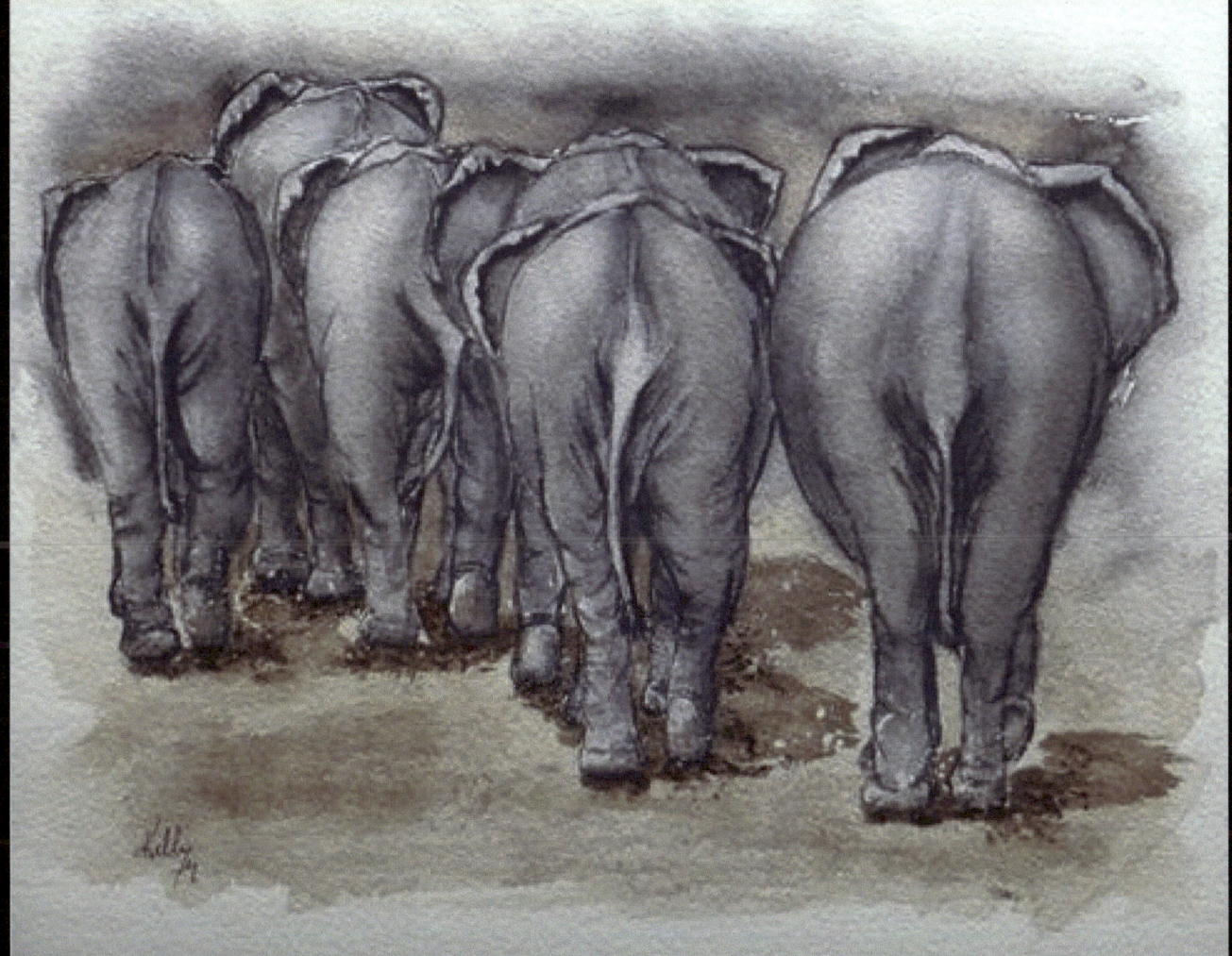

Original 14"x 11" Watercolor

Horse's Side

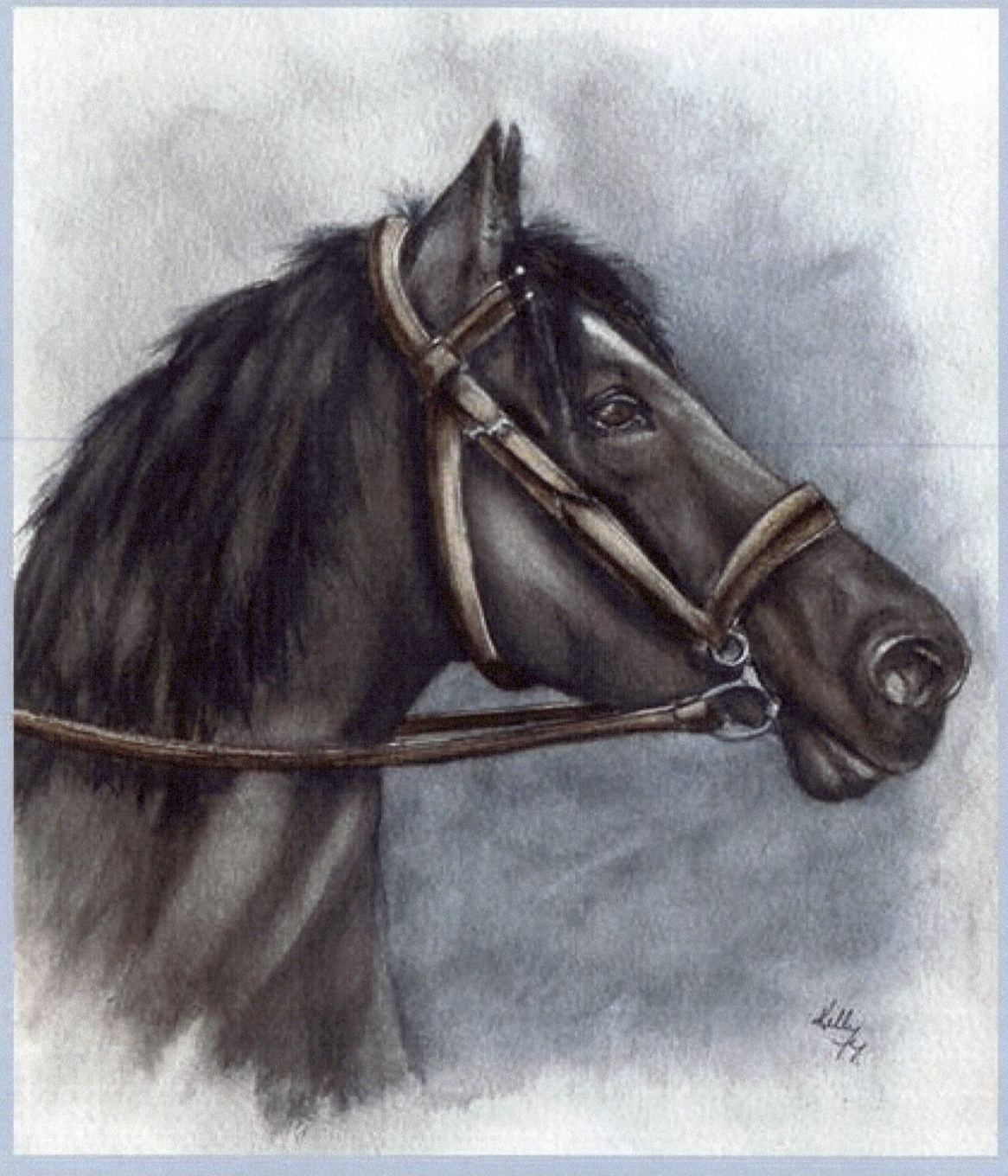

Original 11"x 14" Watercolor

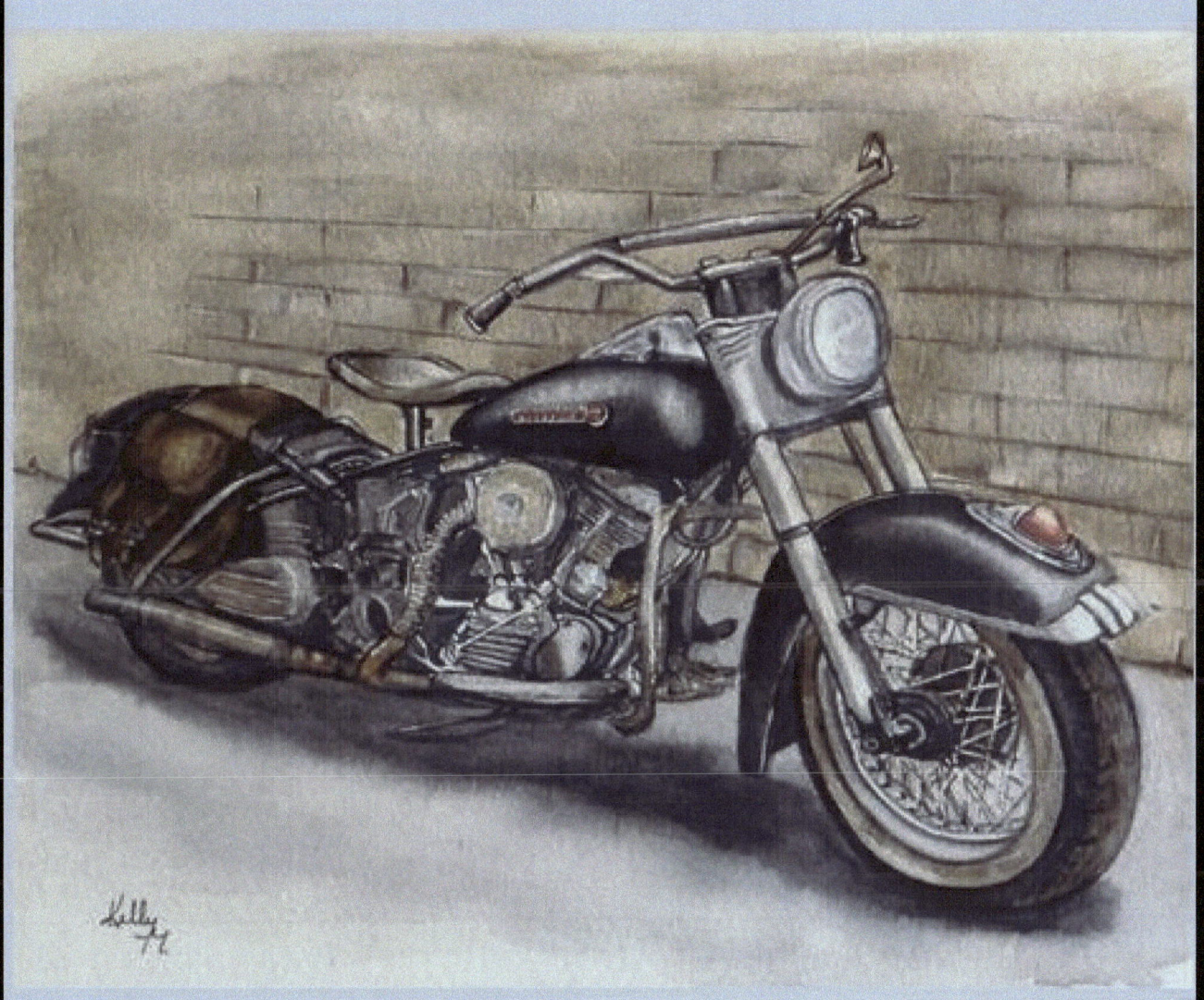

Elephant's Eye

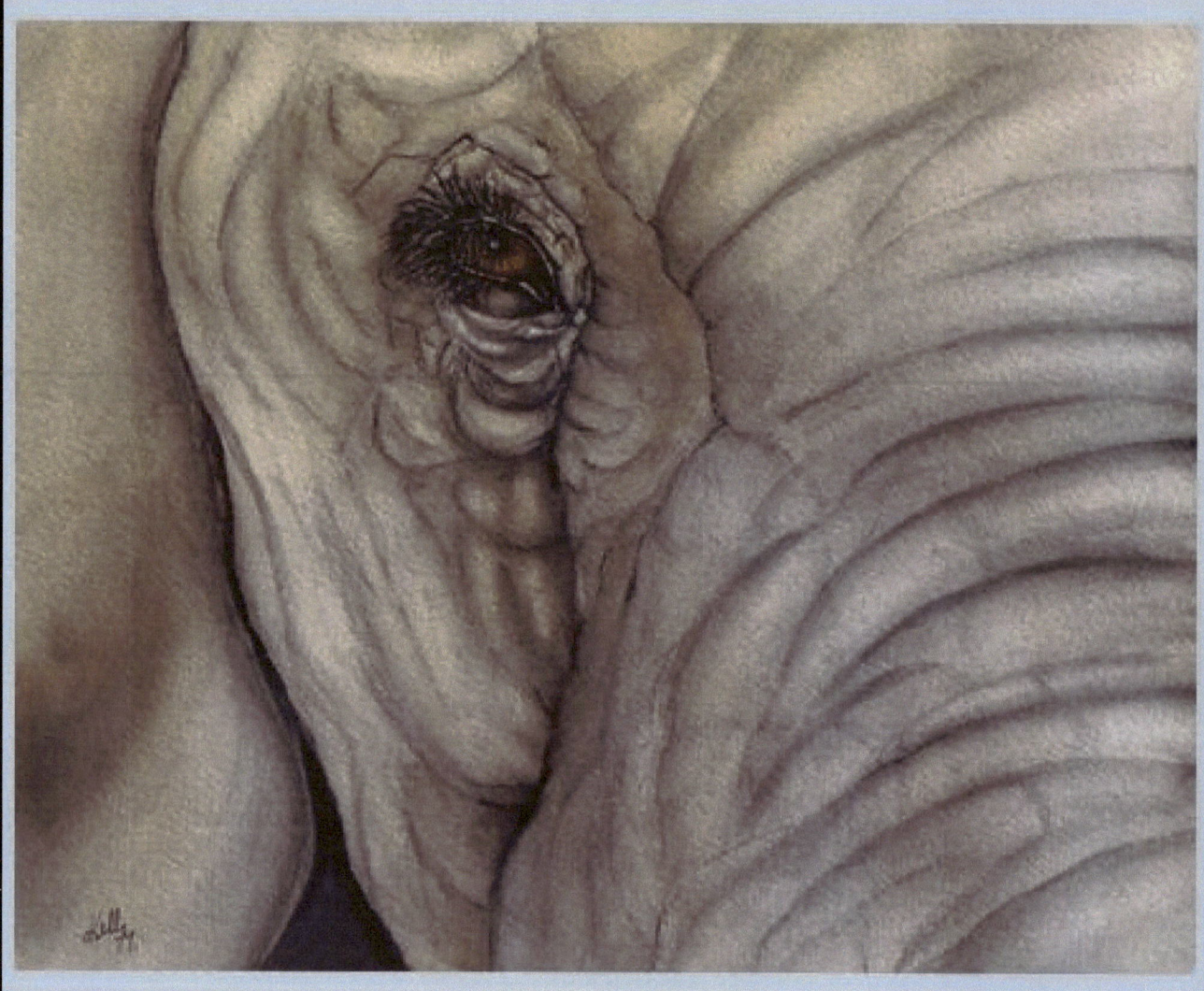

Original 14"x 11" Watercolor

Umbrella Infinity Walk

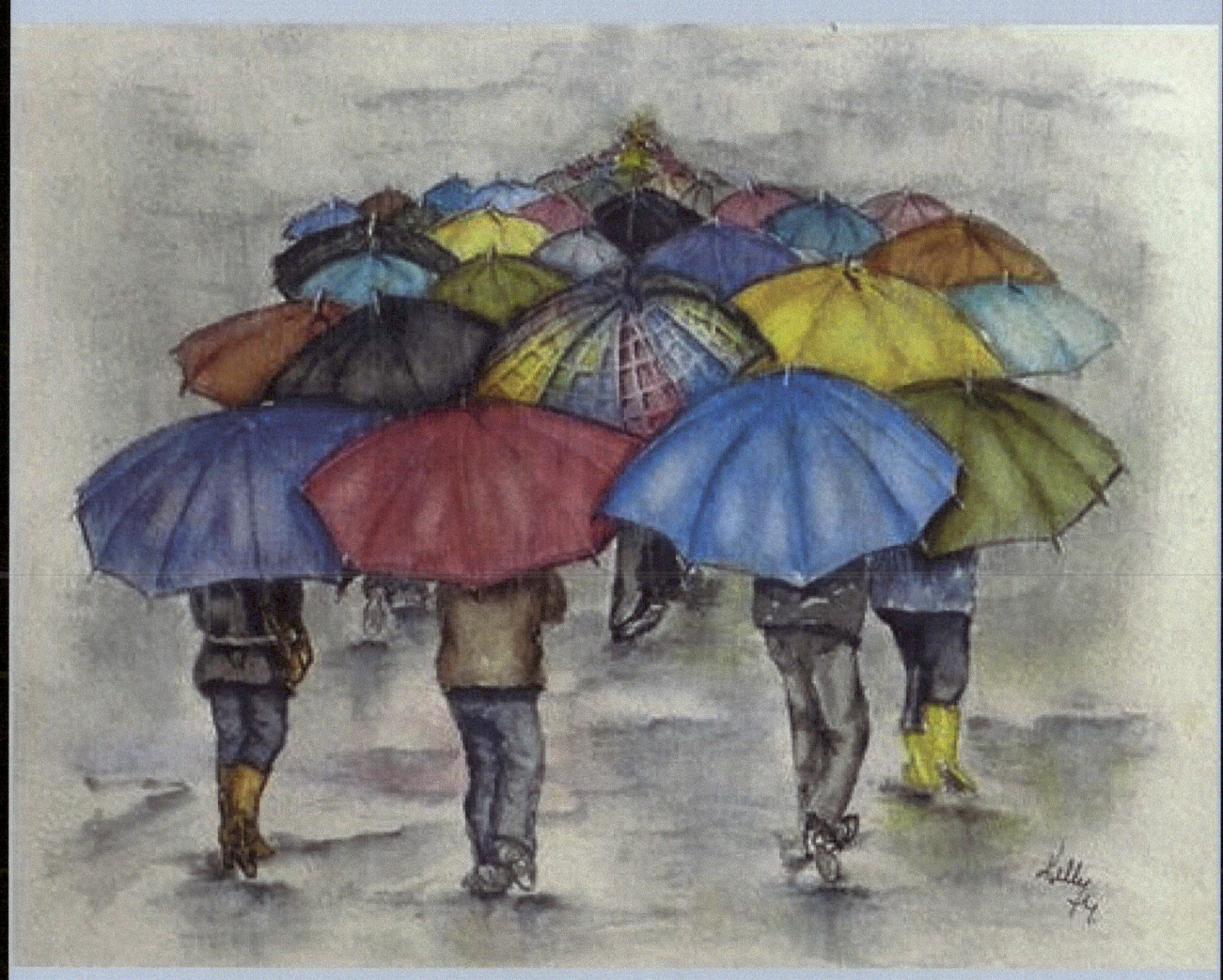

Original 14"x 11" Watercolor

African elephant

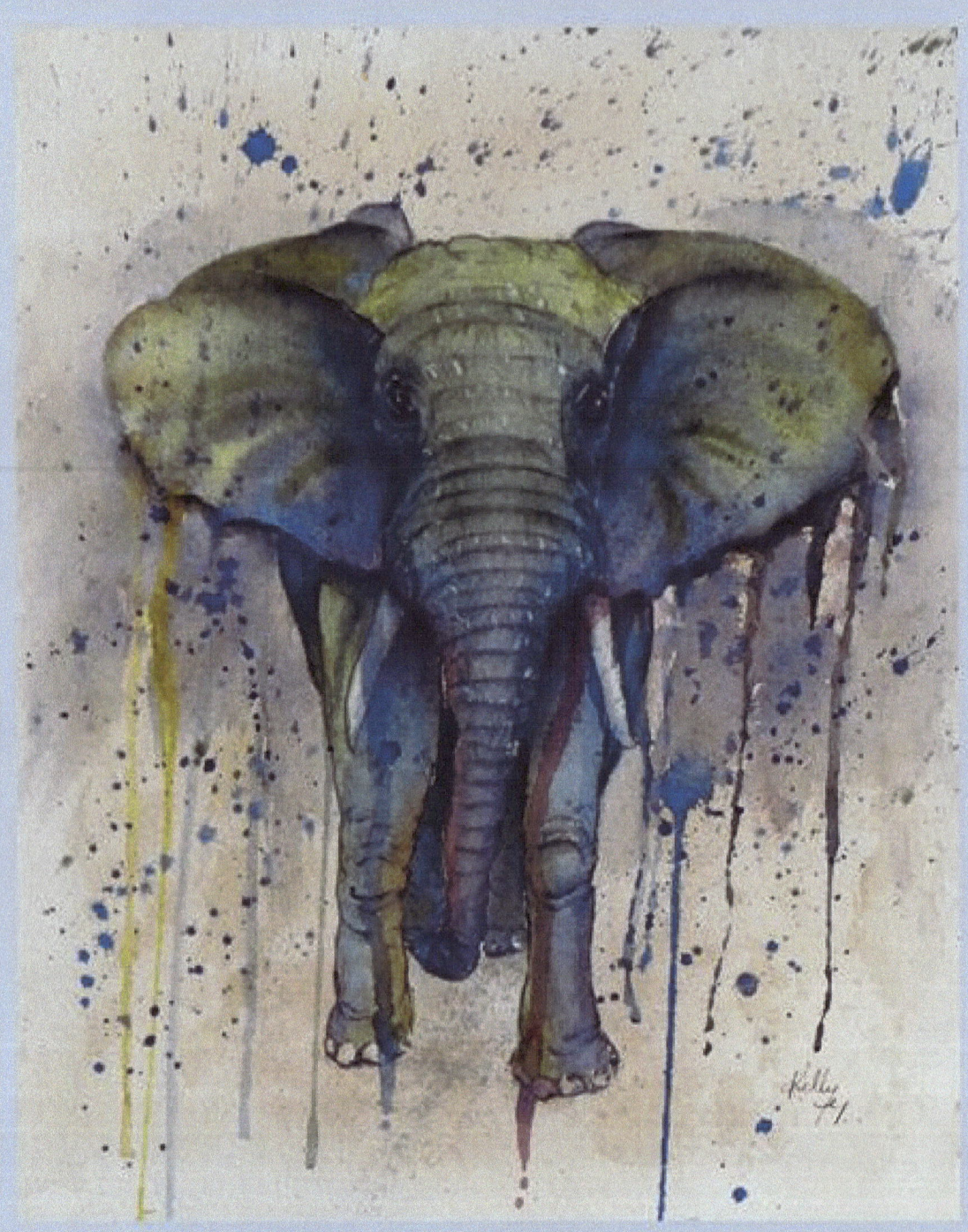

Original 11"x 14" Watercolor

Shirley Temple

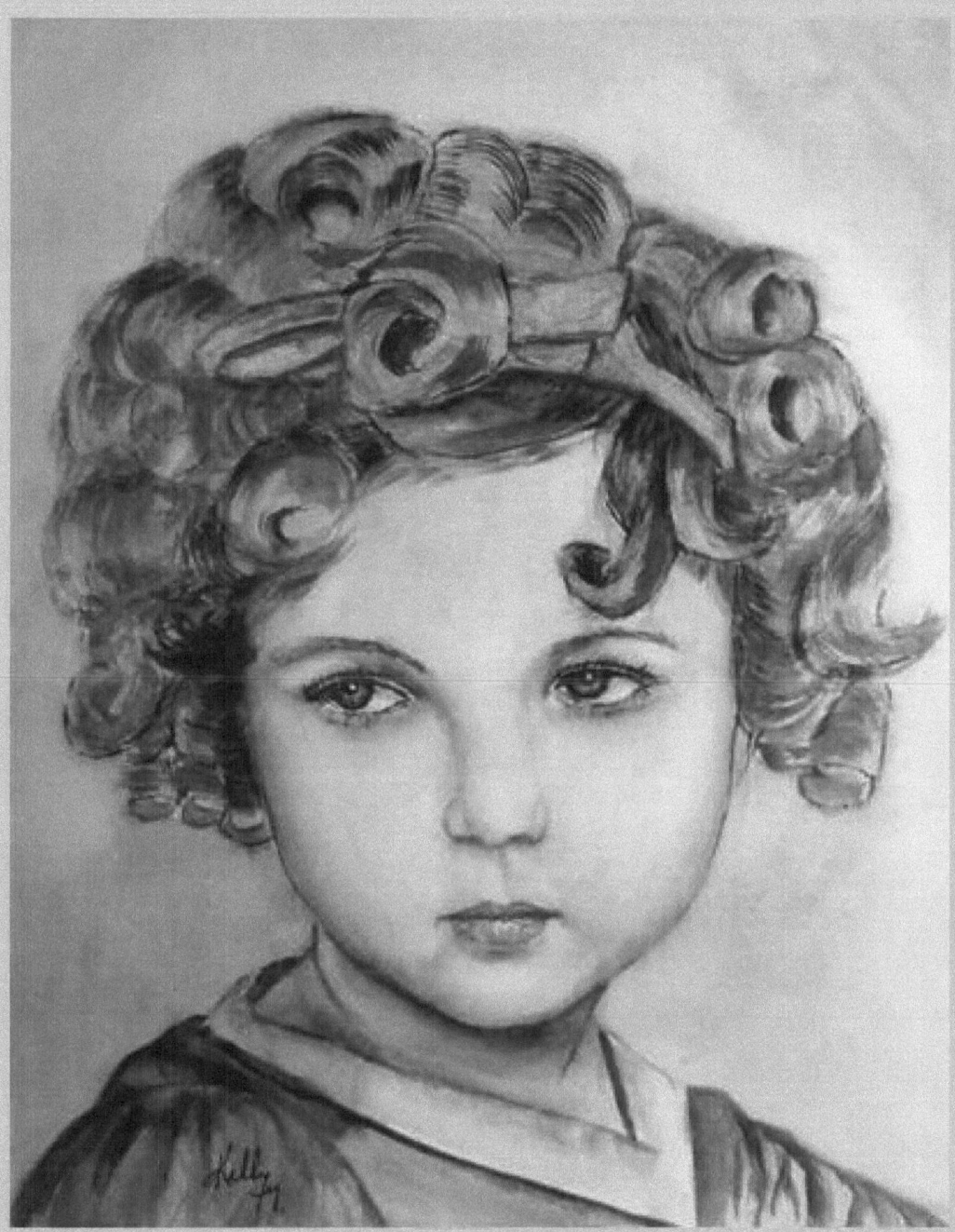

Original 11"x 14" Watercolor

Fashion 2020

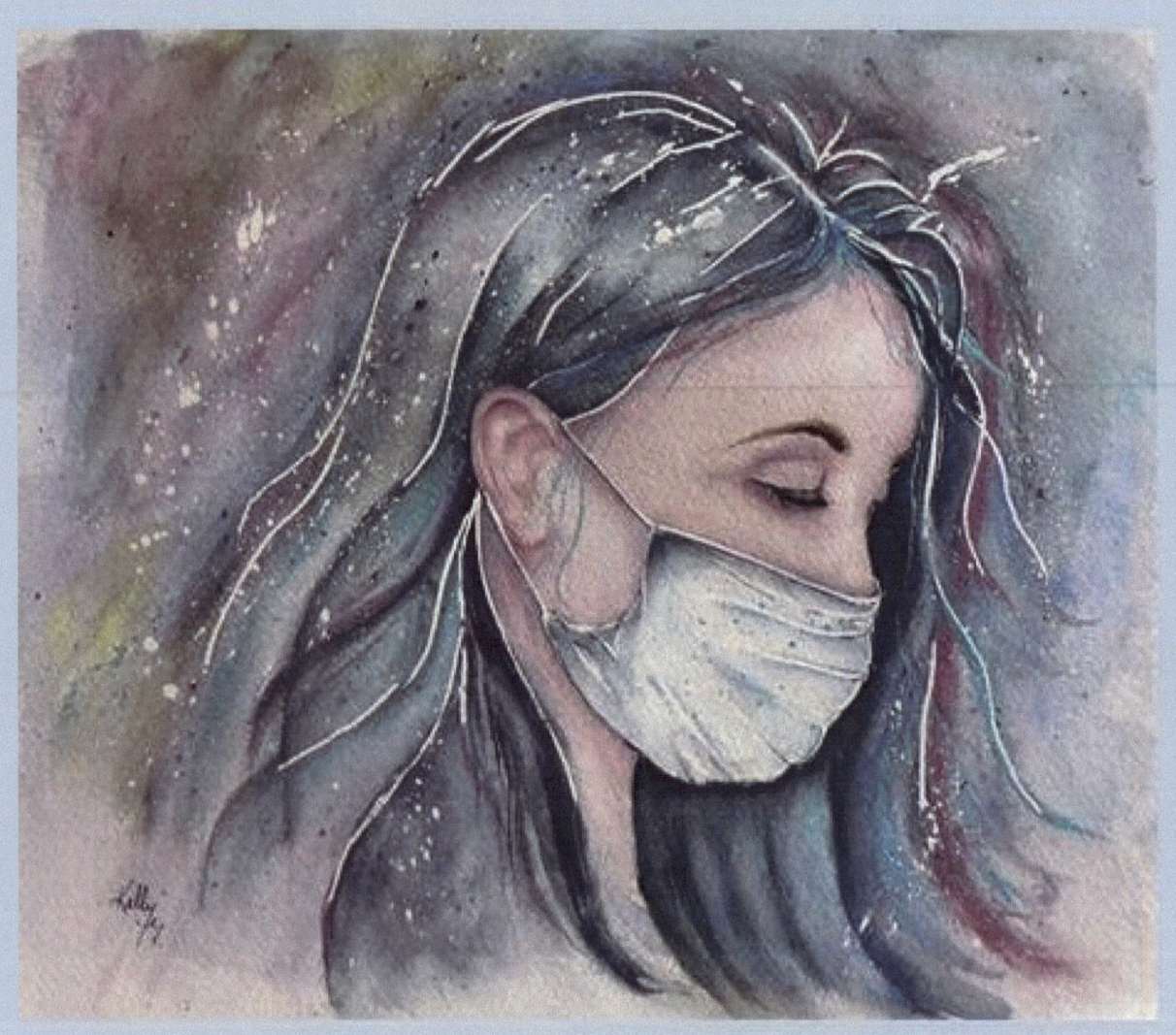

Original 14"x 11" Watercolor

Strumming on the Ol' Banjo

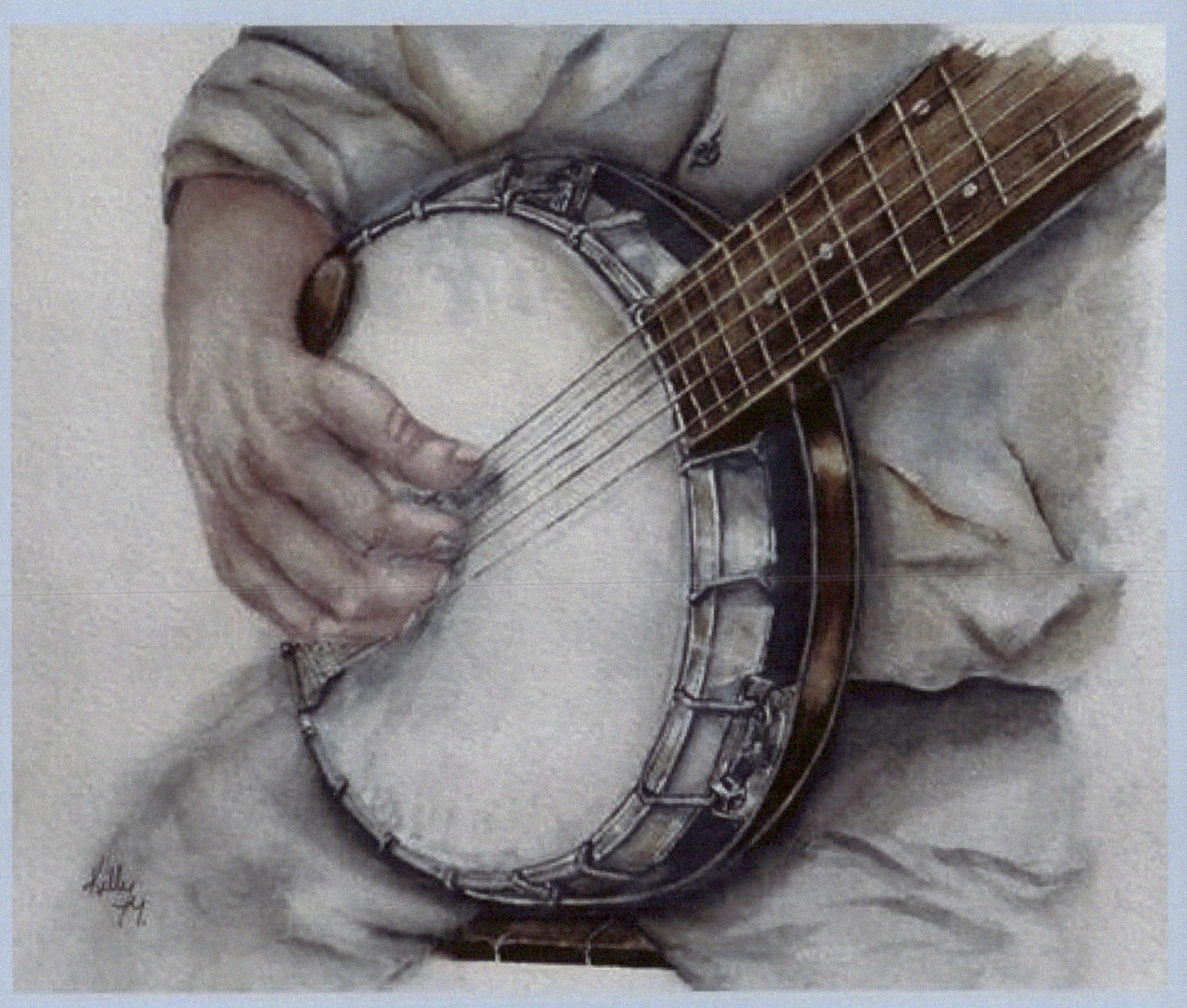

Original 14"x 11" Watercolor

Vintage Gramophone

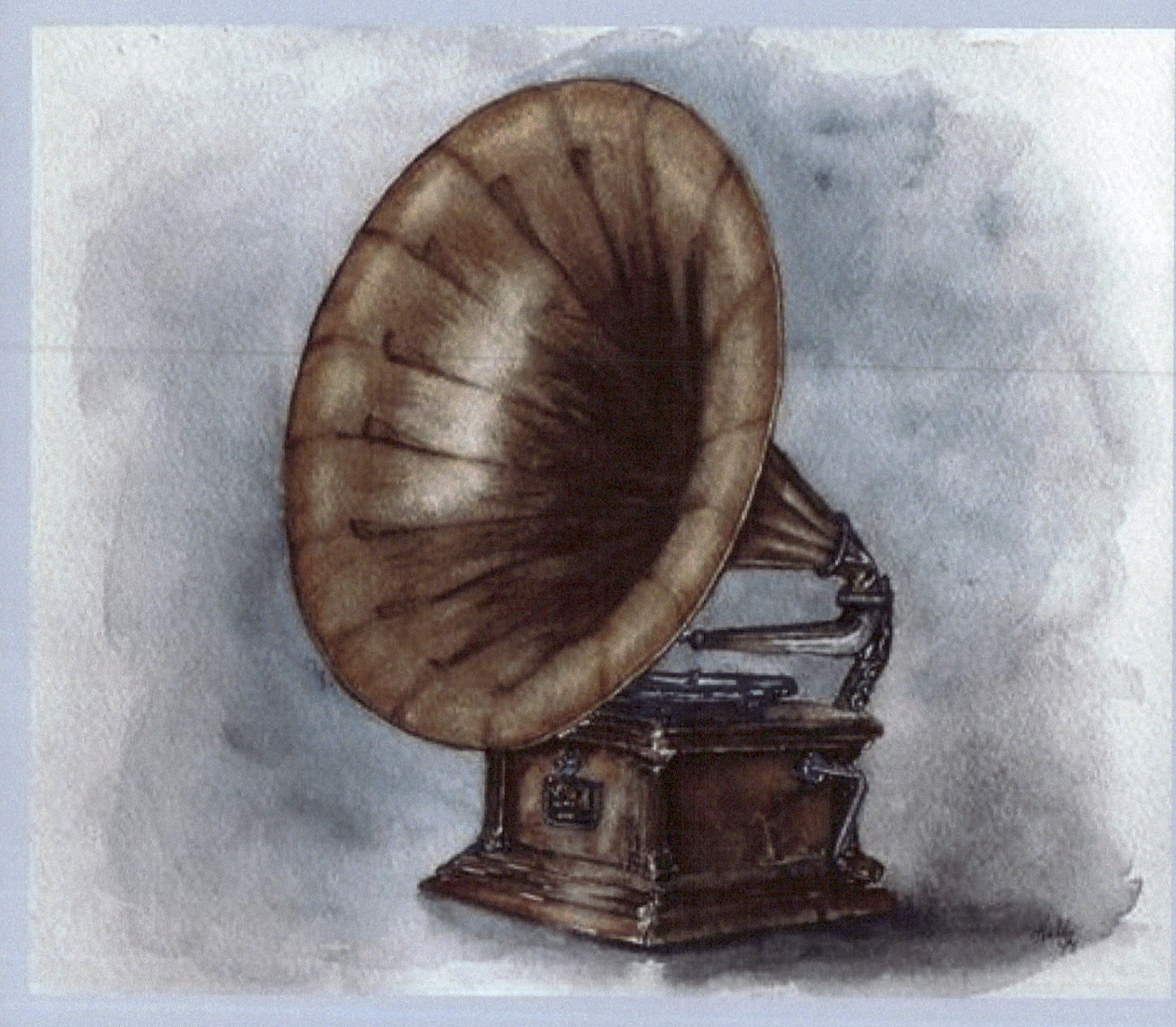

Original 14"x 11" Watercolor

Proud Peacock

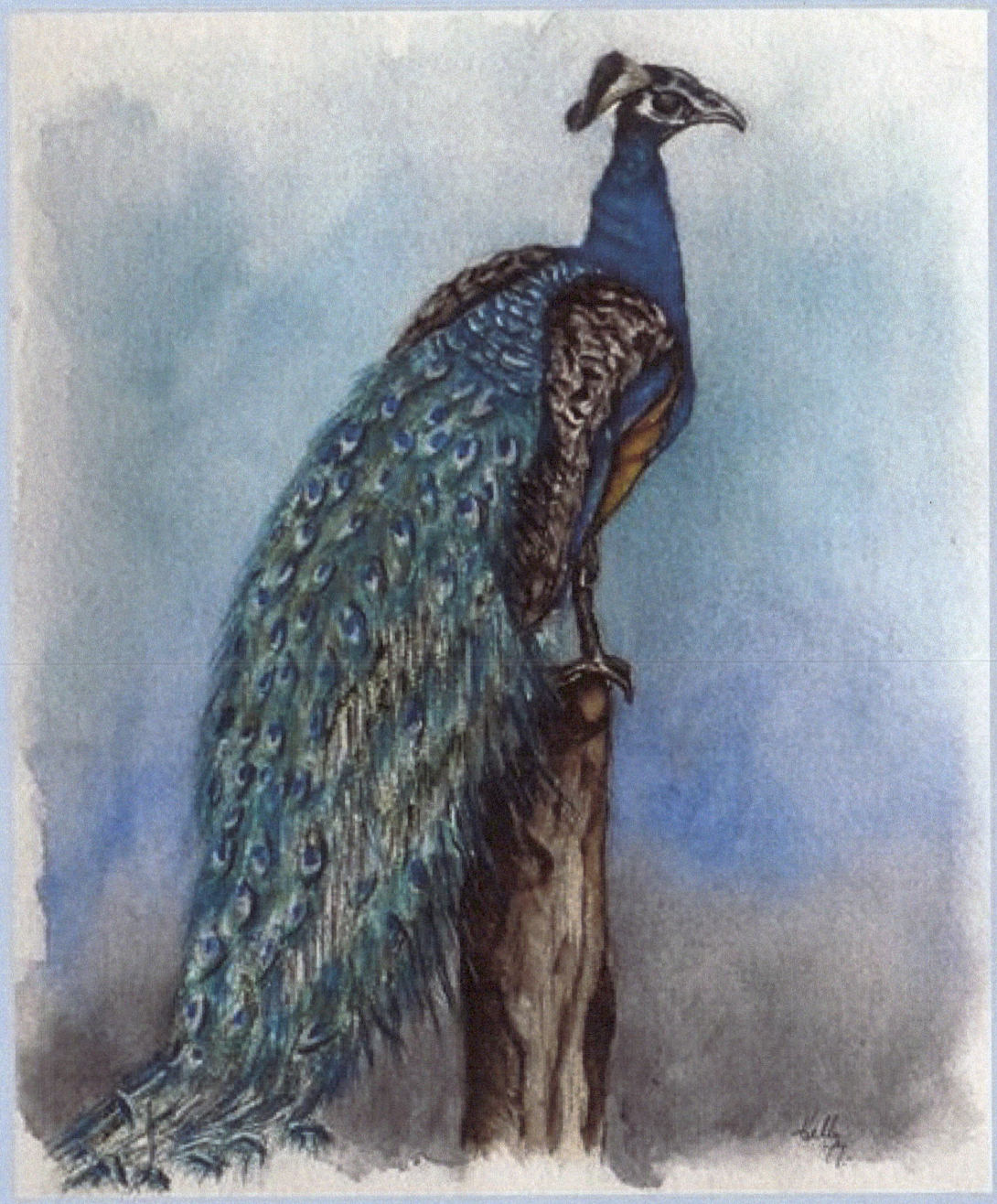

Original 11"x 14" Watercolor

Red Tie

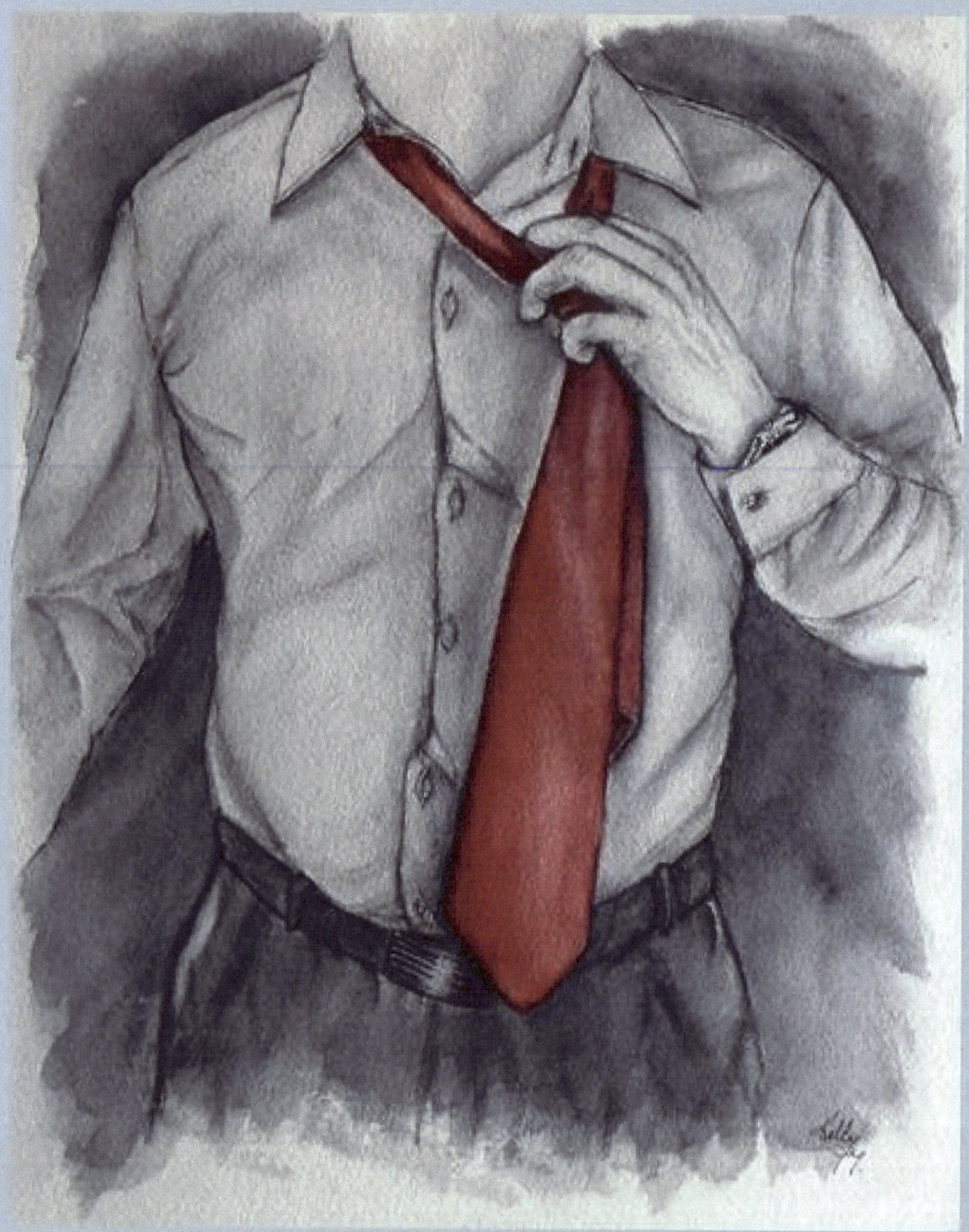

Original 11"x 14" Watercolor

Shhh Tiger Cub is Sleeping

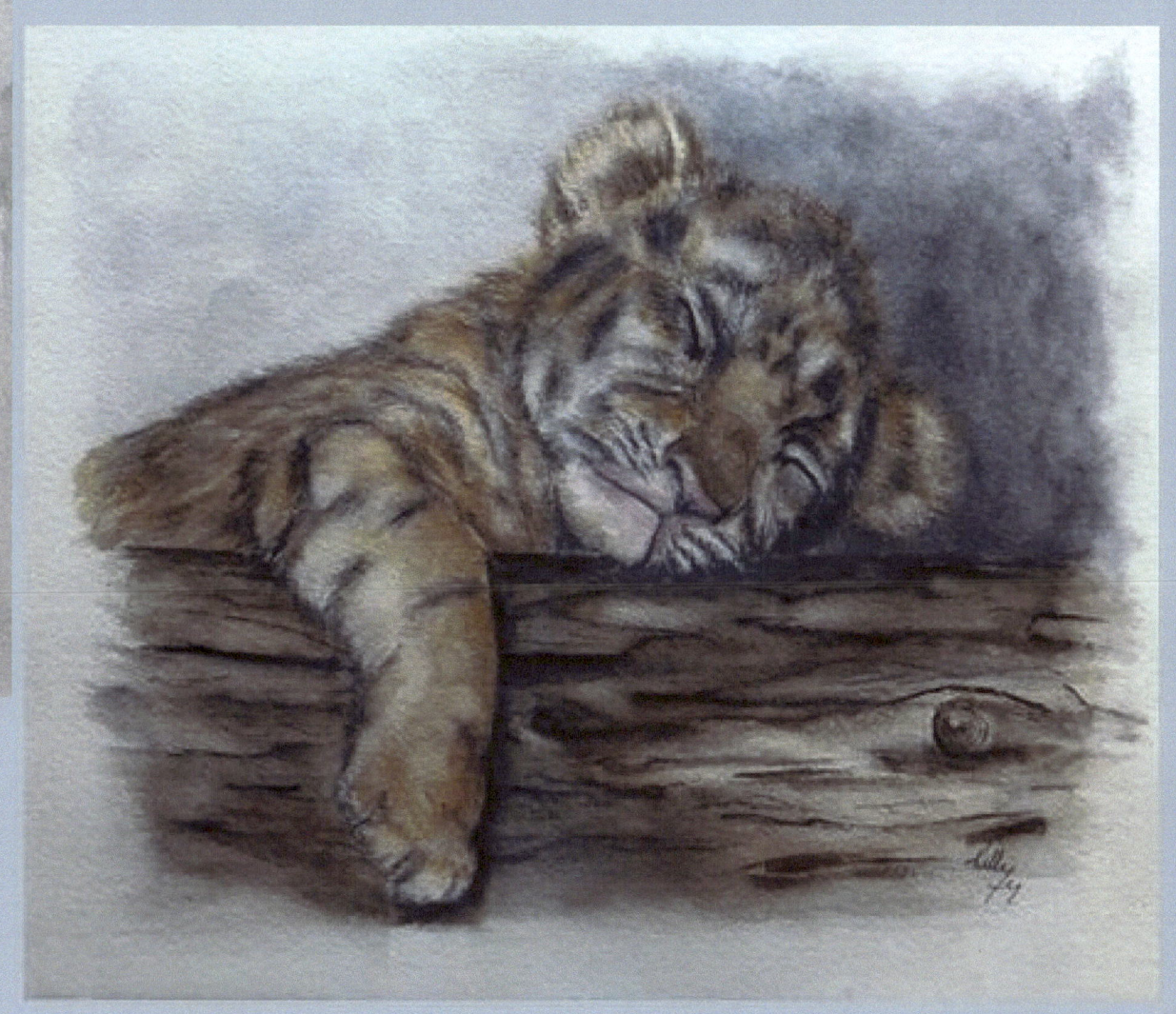

Original 14"x 11" Watercolor

Mama & Baby Giraffe

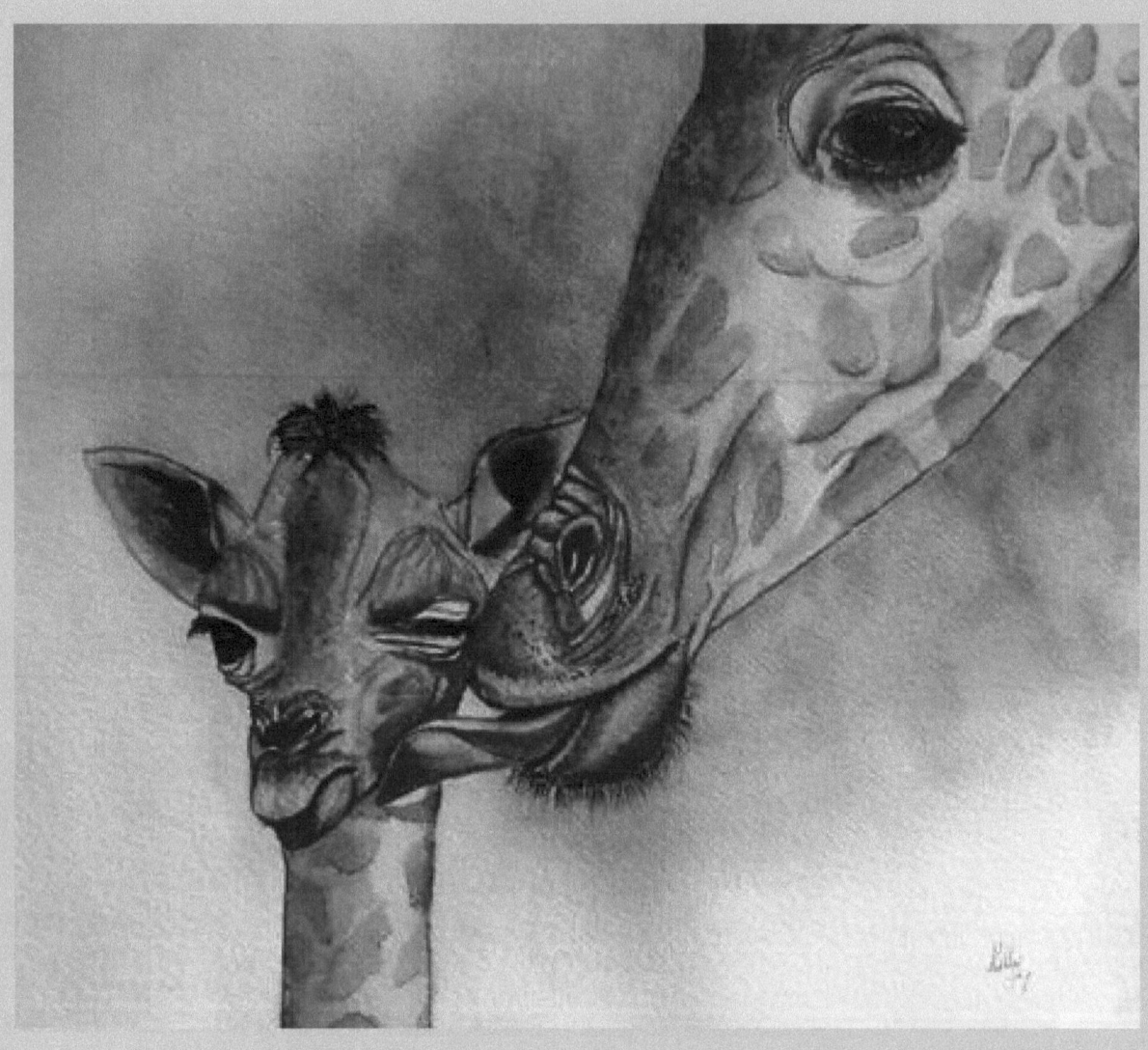

Original 14"x 11" Watercolor

Vintage Baseball Glove

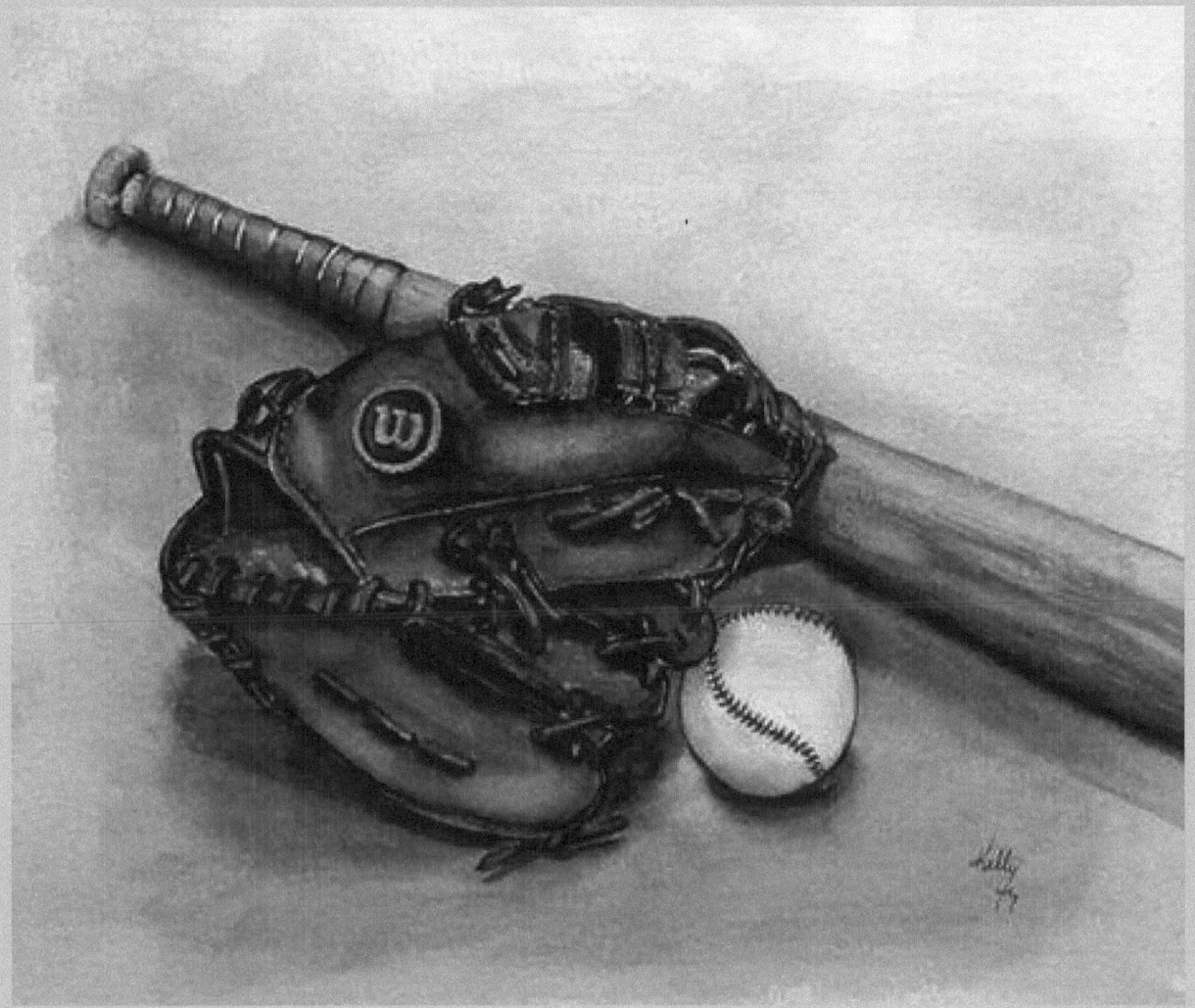

Original 14"x 11" Watercolor

Red Heels & Jeans

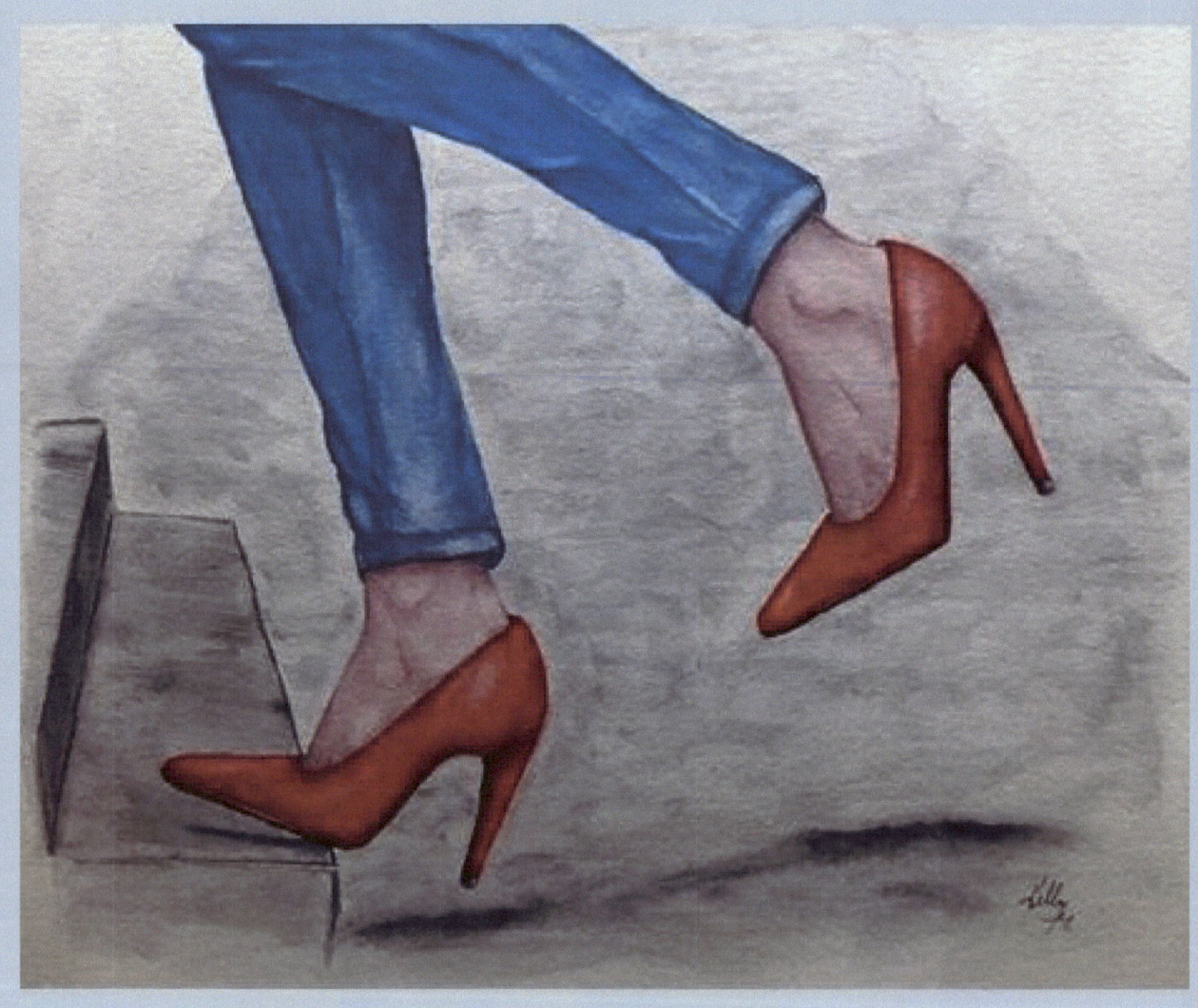

Original 14"x 11" Watercolor

Majestic Roar

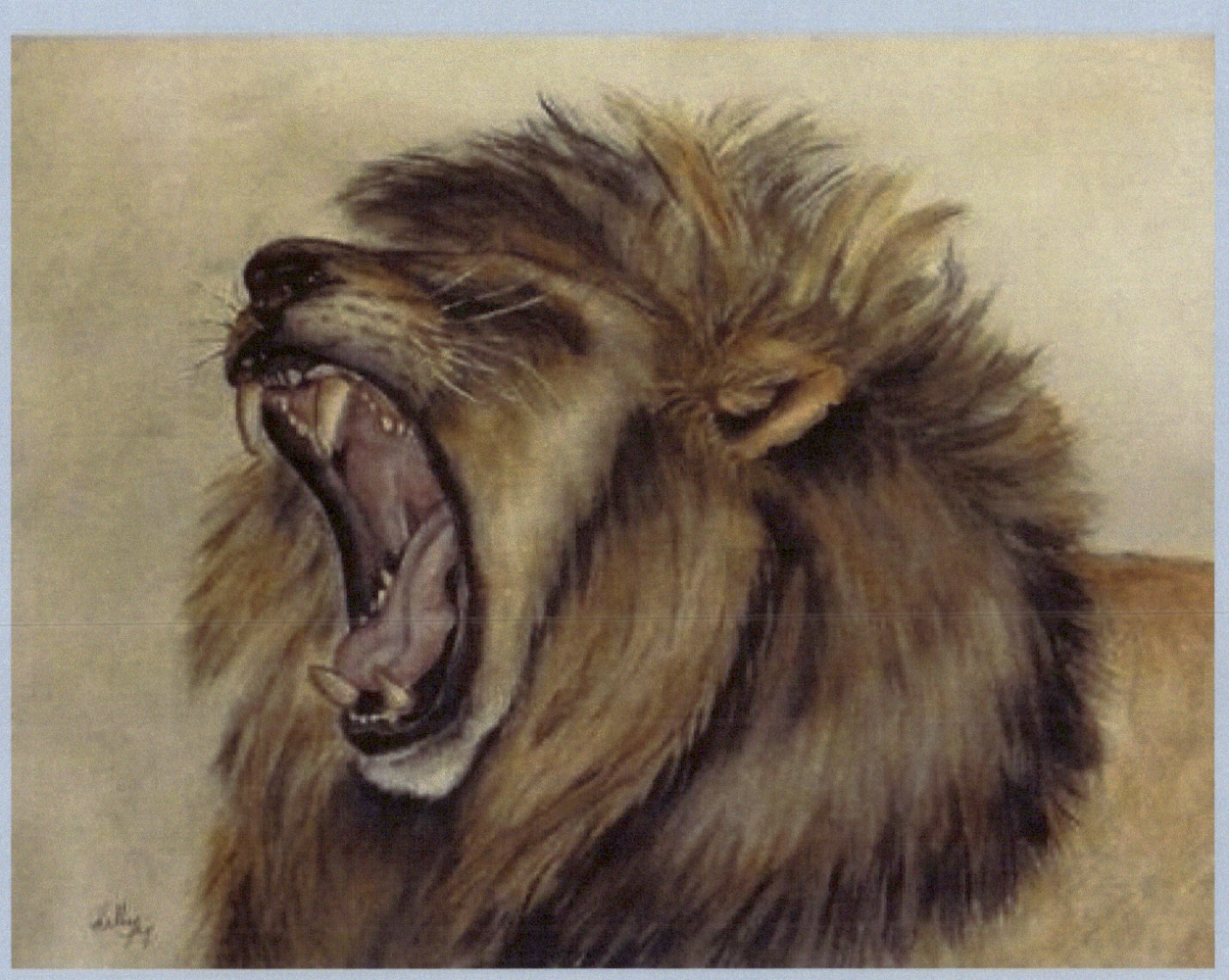

Original 14"x 11" Watercolor

Daisy-A-Day

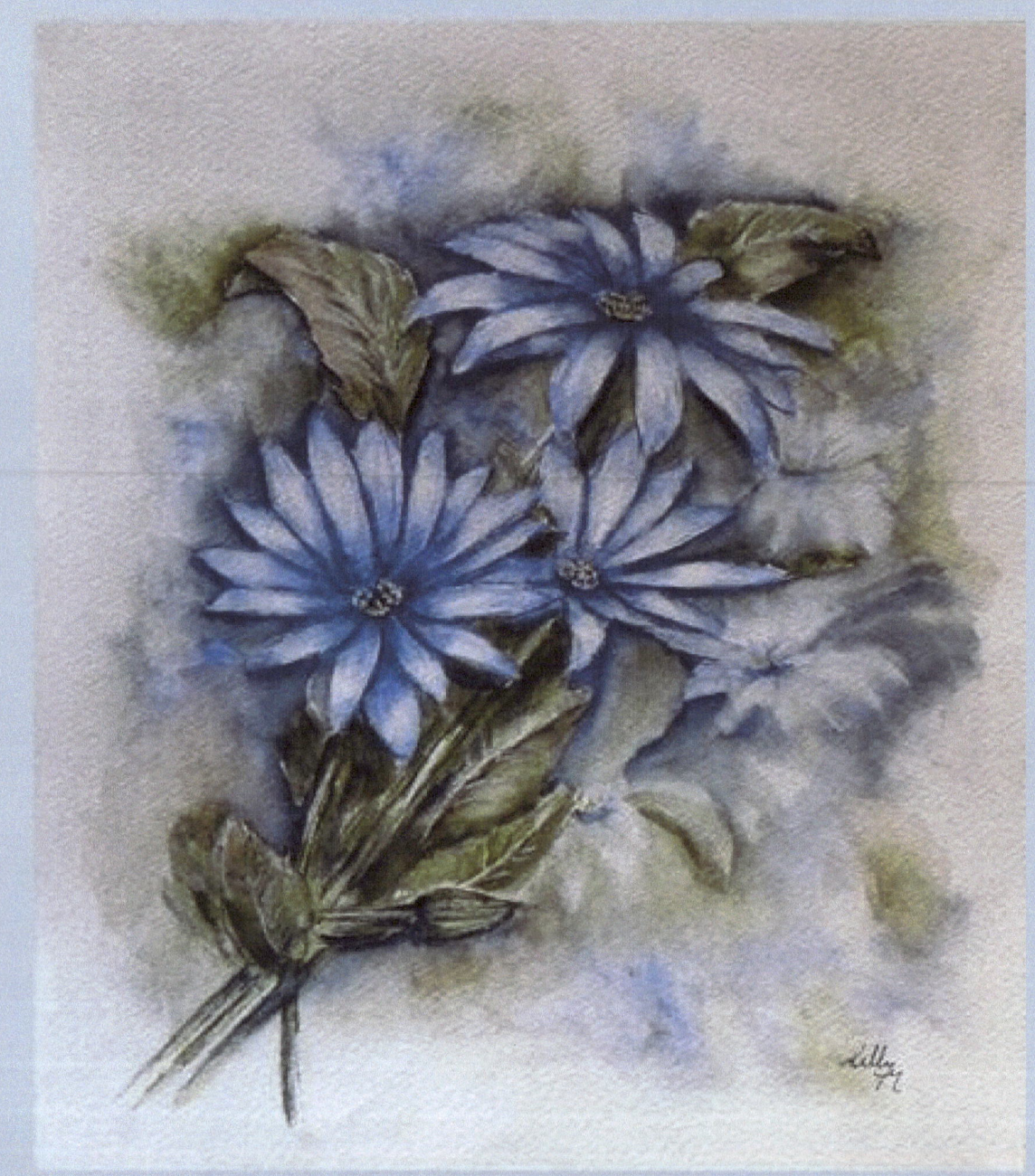

Original 11"x 14" Watercolor

Oversized Umbrella

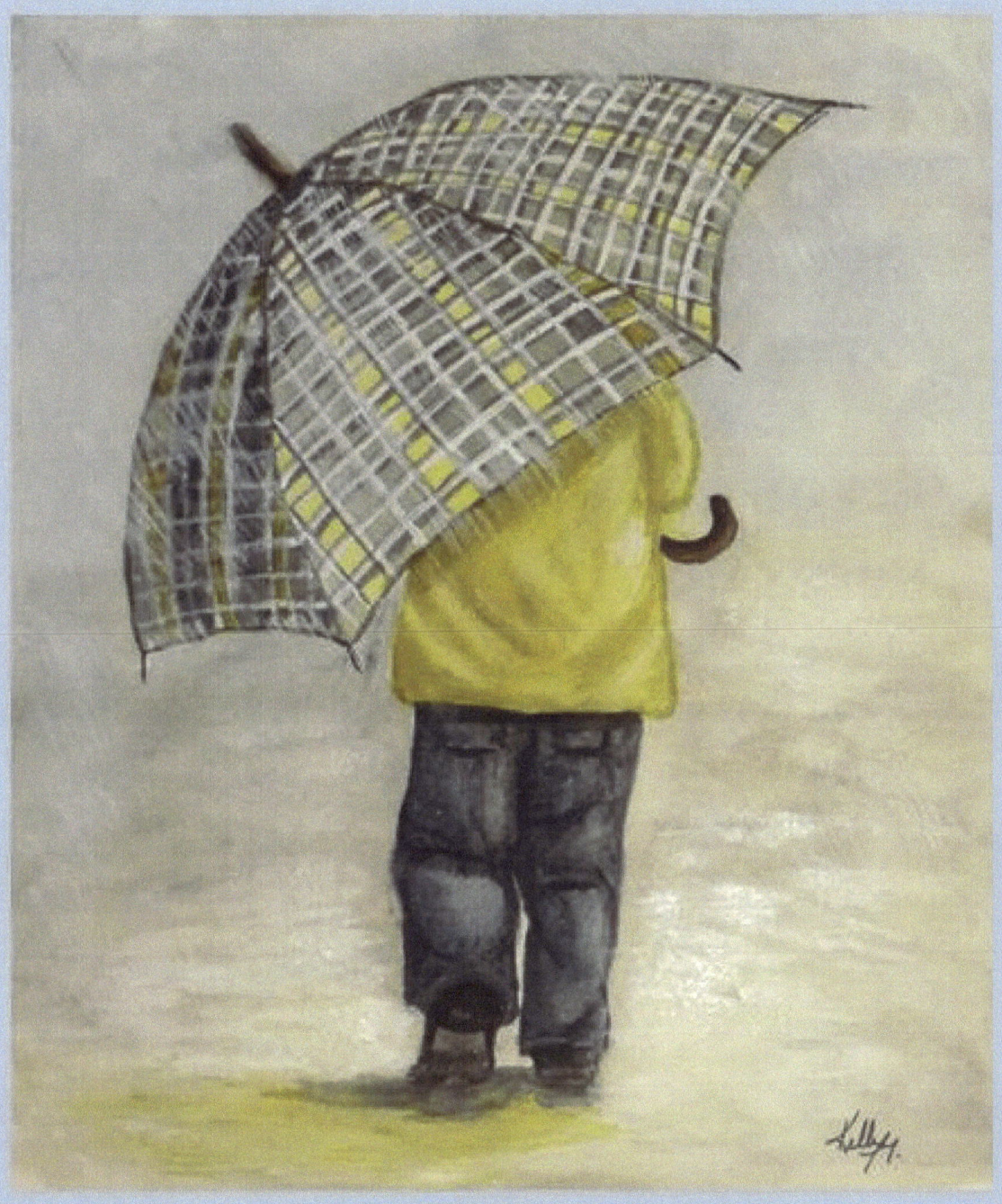

Original 11"x 14" Watercolor

Bicycle in Red

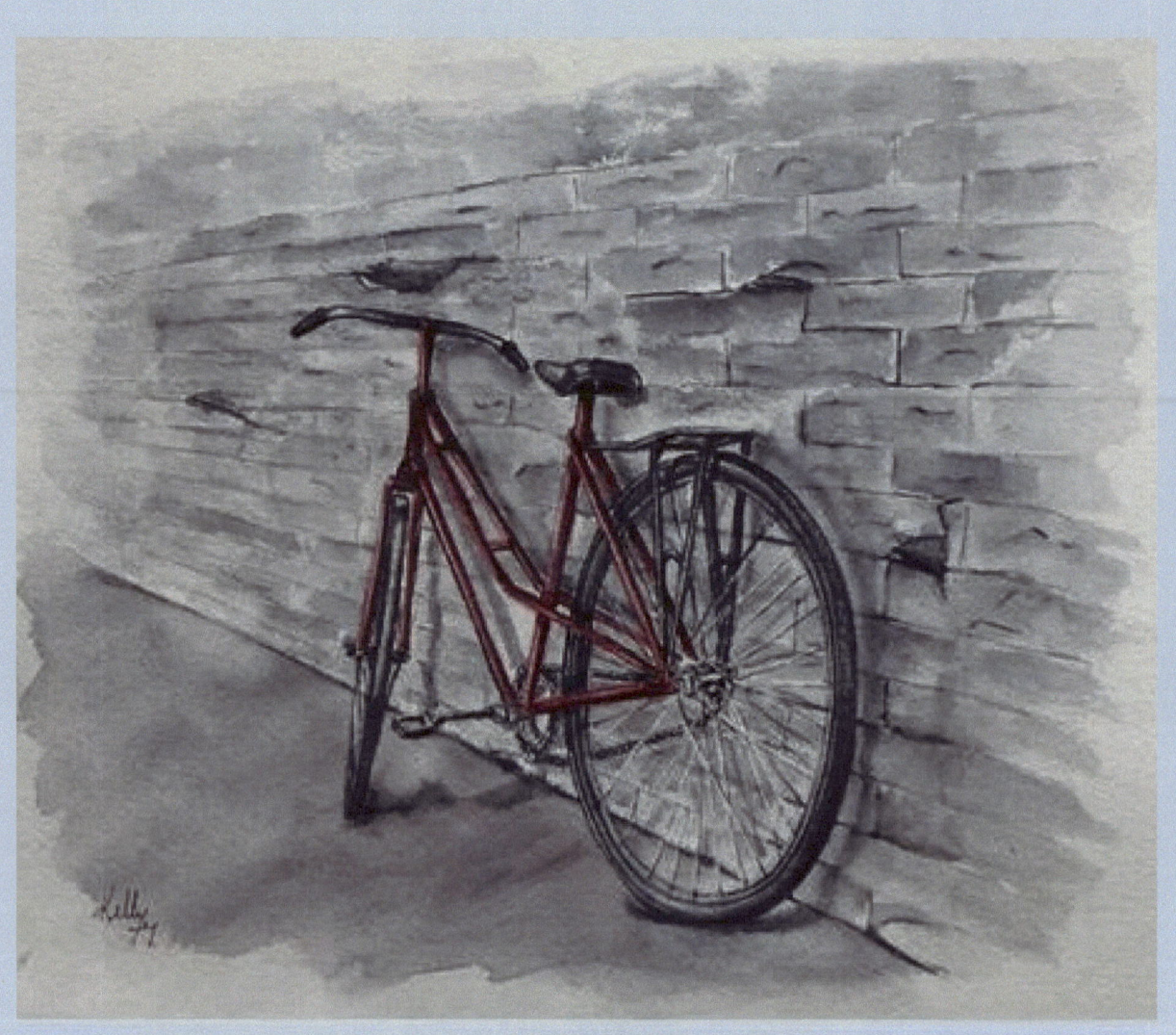

Original 14"x 11" Watercolor

1950's Vingtage Harley

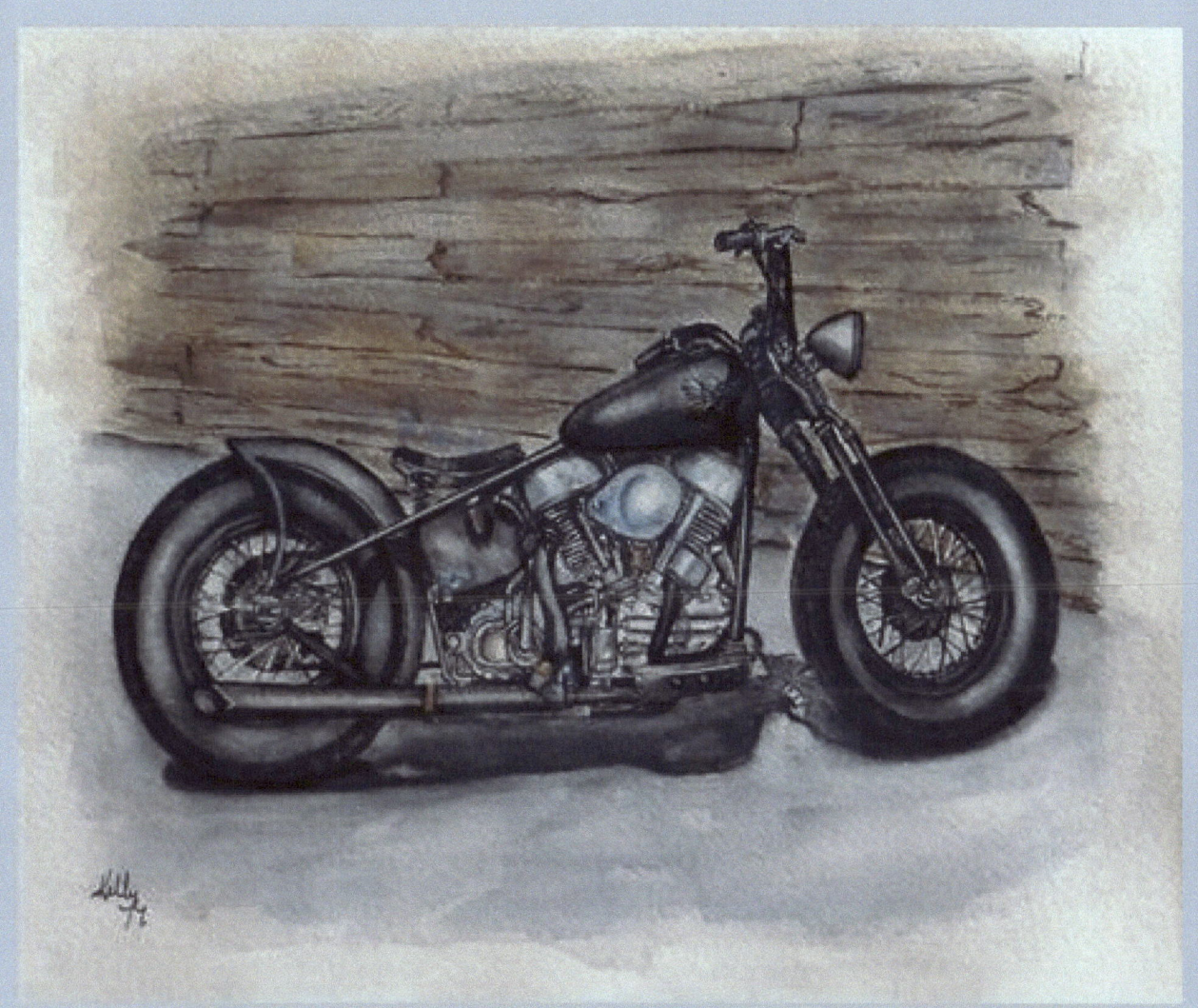

Original 14"x 11" Watercolor

Red Wolf

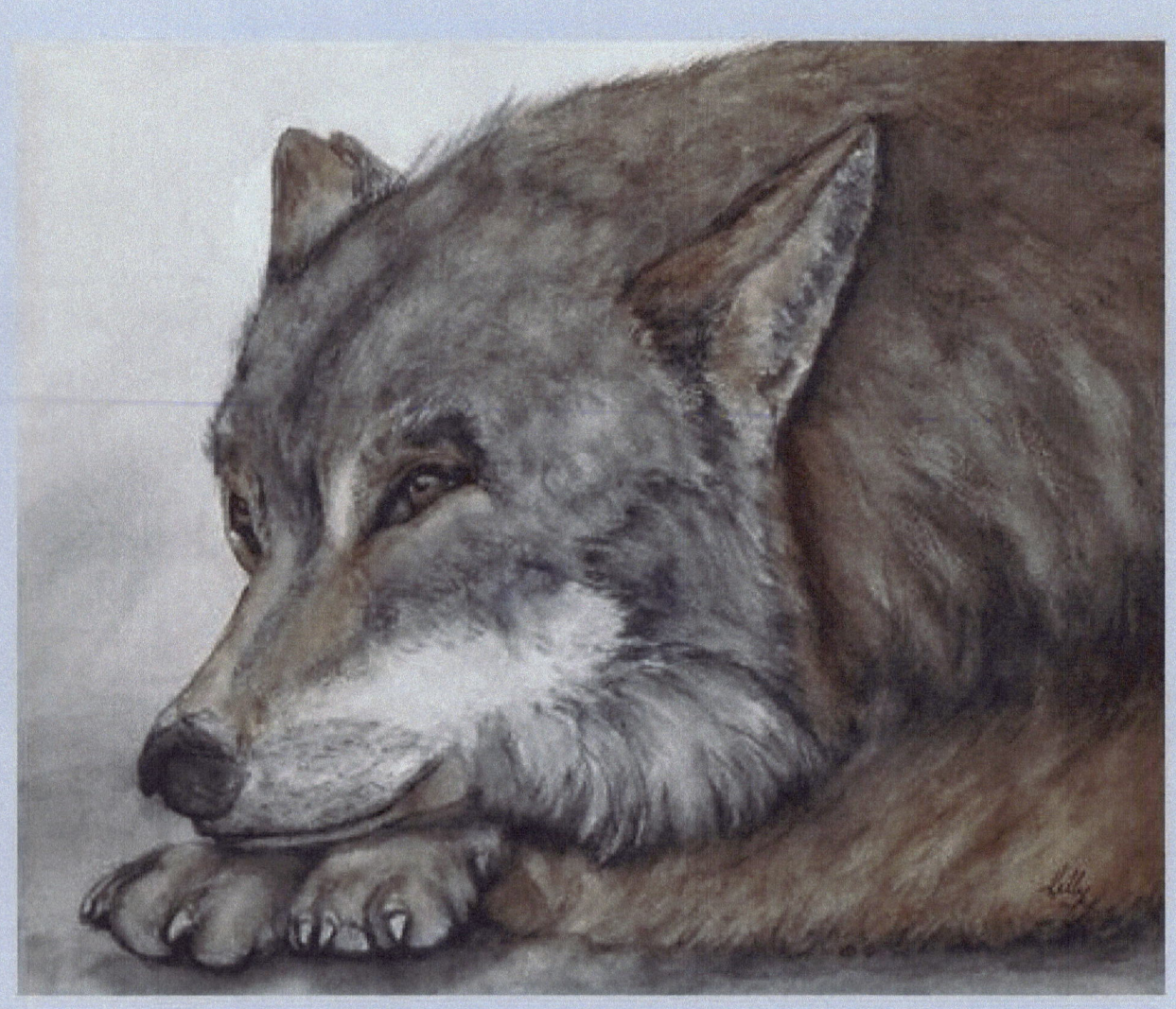

Original 14"x 11" Watercolor

Newborn Giraffe

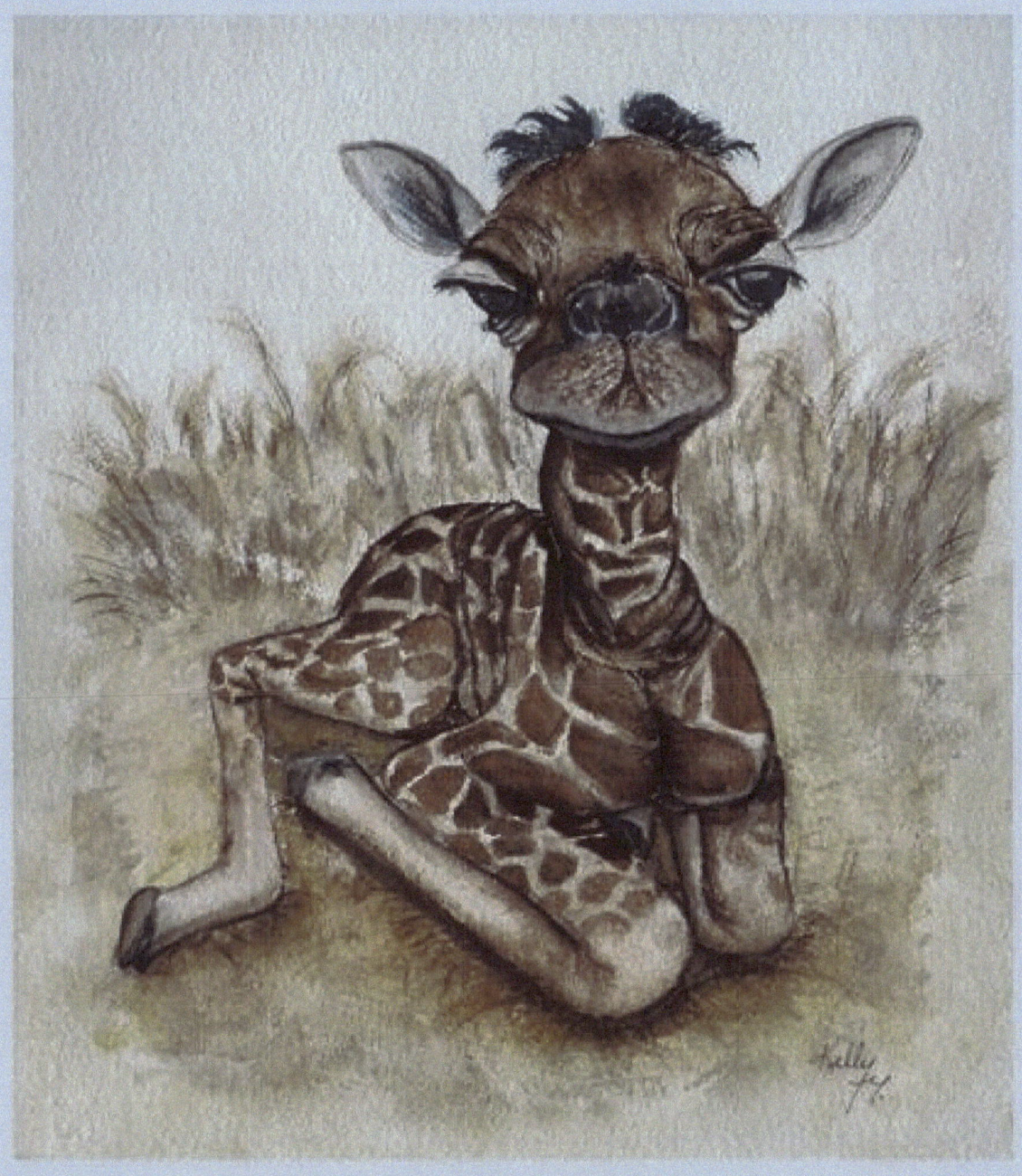

Original 11"x 14" Watercolor

Junior Fishing

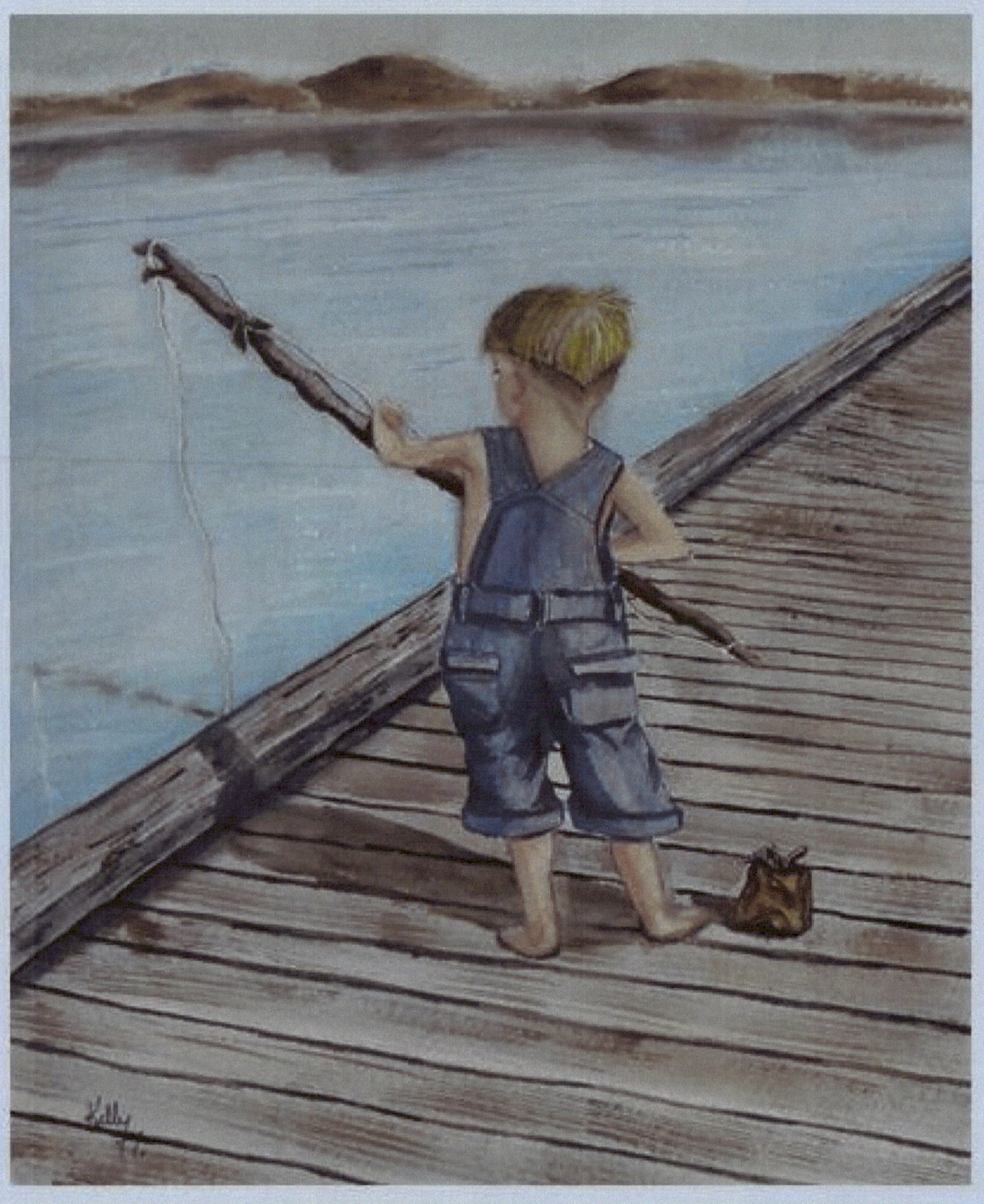

Original 11"x 14" Watercolor

An Orange

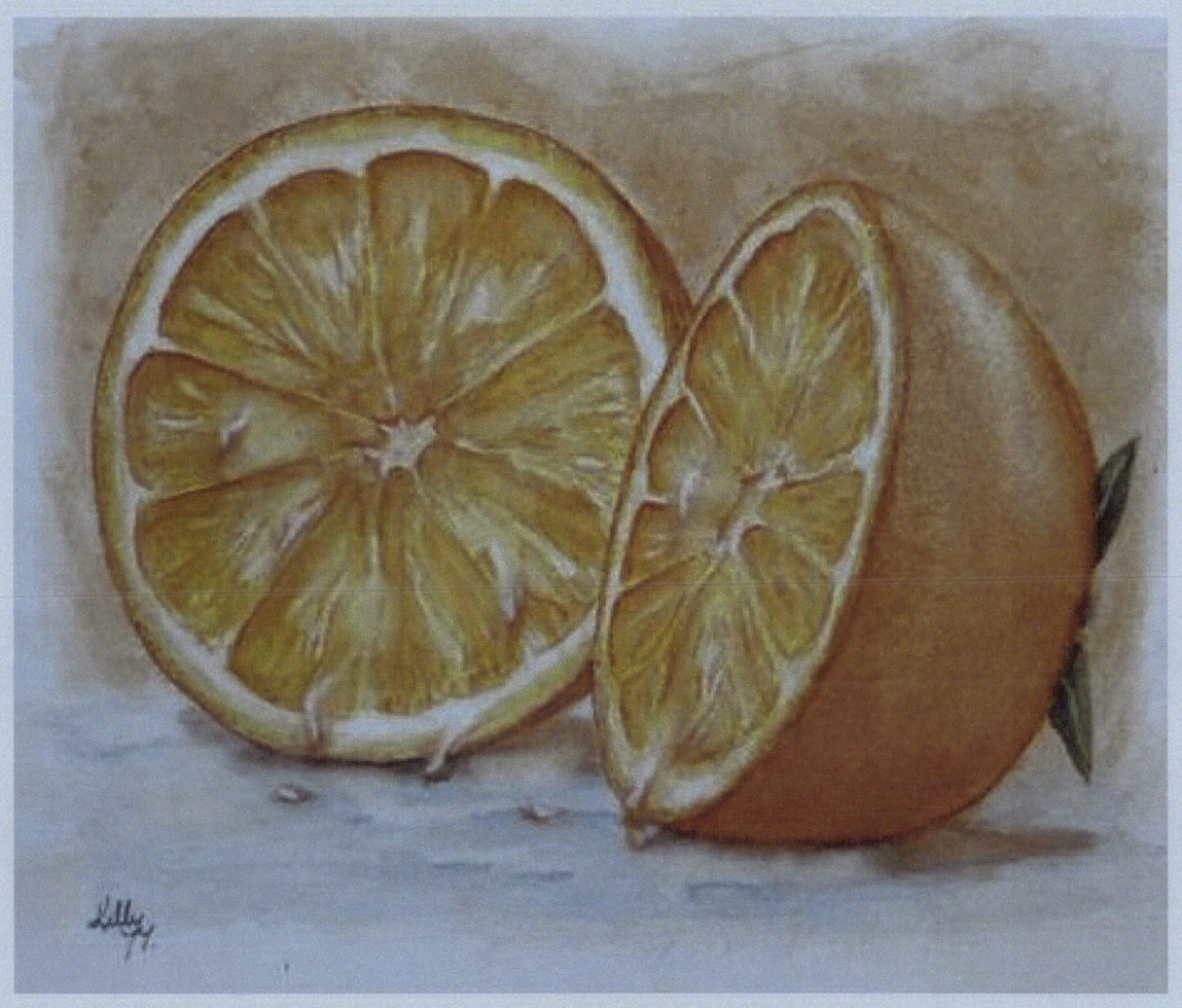

Original 14"x 11" Watercolor

Copper Stair Case

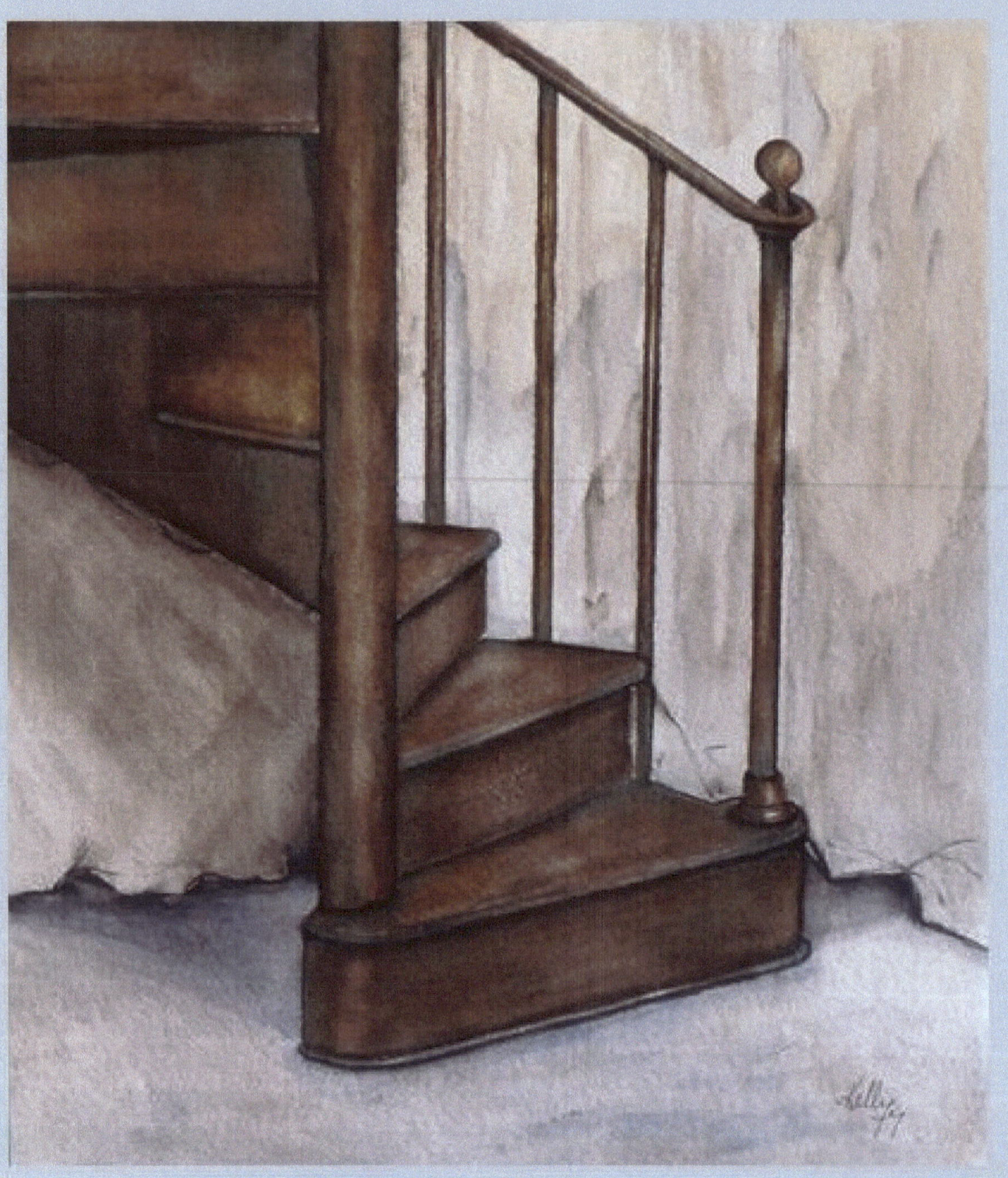

Original 11"x 14" Watercolor

Antler Shuffle

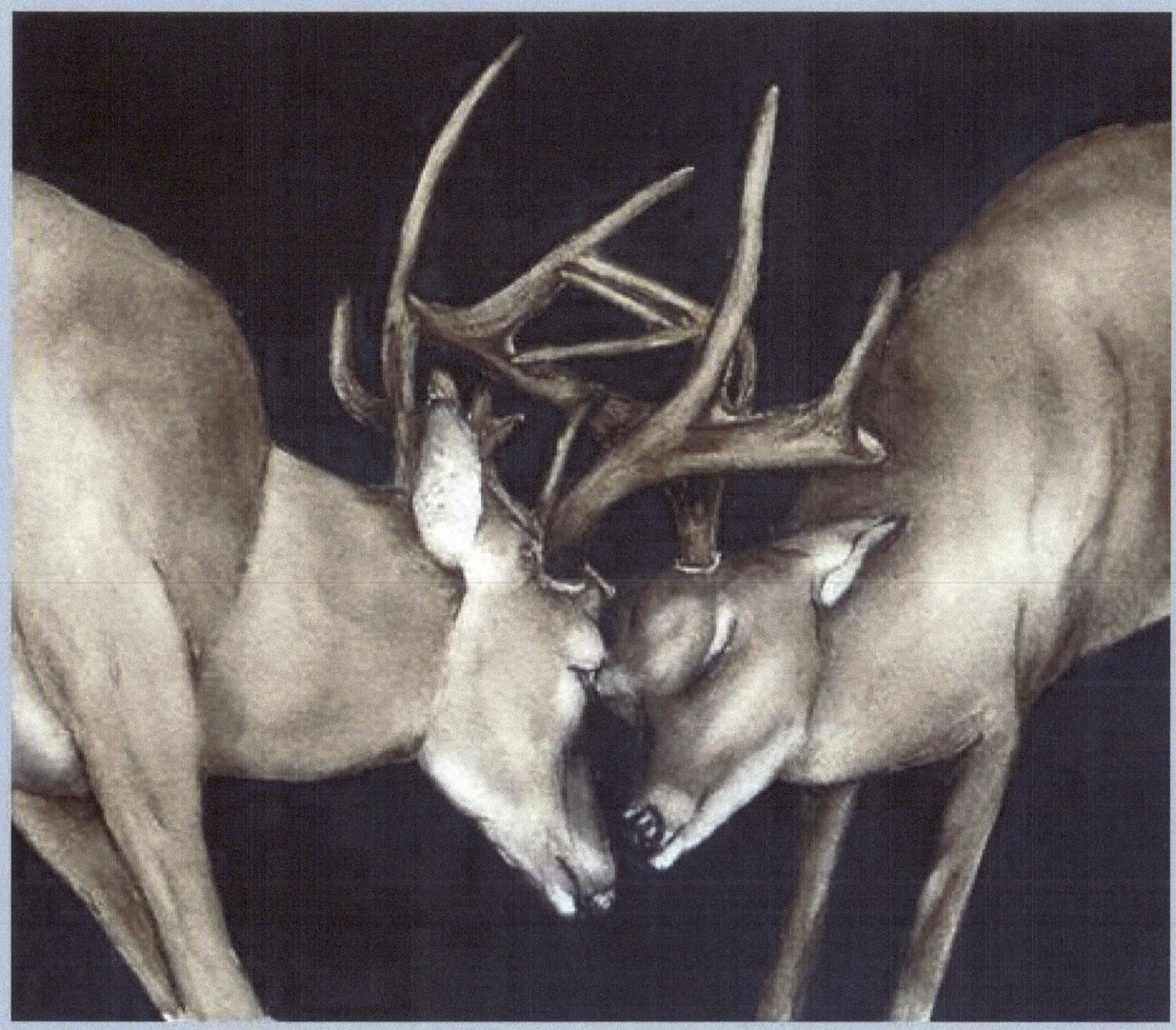

Original 14"x 11" Watercolor

The Handshake

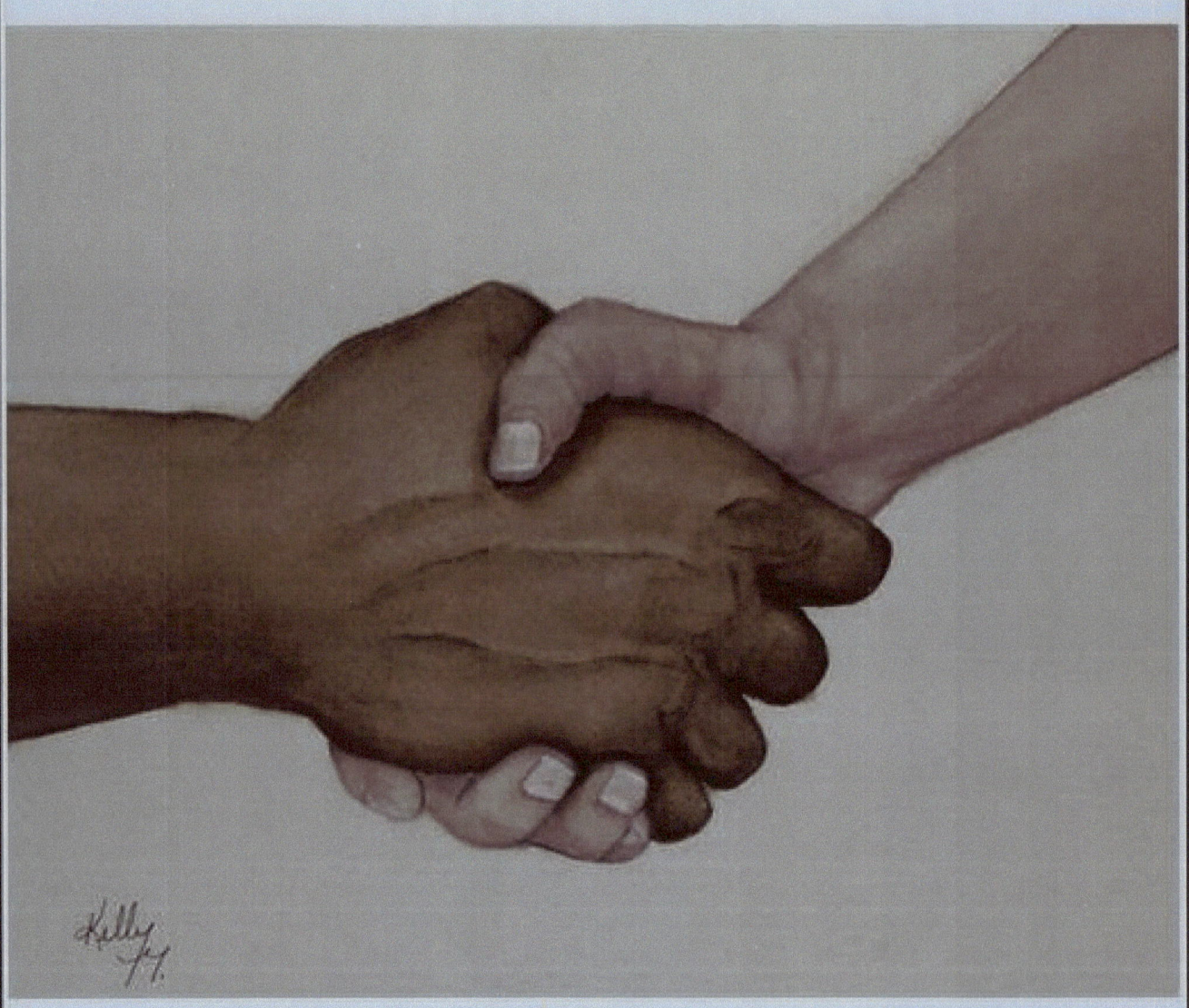

Kelly Mills Watercolor Paintings are found at:
www.watercolormemories-kellym.com

Original 10"x 8" Watercolor

www.ingramcontent.com/pod-product-compliance
Lightning Source LLC
Chambersburg PA
CBHW040419220526
45473CB00004B/1287